T0323960

ASSESSING AND INSURING CYBERSECURITY RISK

ASSESSING AND INSURING CYBERSECURITY RISK

Ravi Das

CRC Press

Taylor & Francis Group

Boca Raton London New York

CRC Press is an imprint of the
Taylor & Francis Group, an **informa** business

AN AUERBACH BOOK

First edition published 2022
by CRC Press
6000 Broken Sound Parkway NW, Suite 300, Boca Raton, FL 33487-2742

and by CRC Press
2 Park Square, Milton Park, Abingdon, Oxon, OX14 4RN

© 2022 Taylor & Francis Group, LLC

CRC Press is an imprint of Taylor & Francis Group, LLC

The right of Ravi Das to be identified as author of this work has been asserted by him in accordance with sections 77 and 78 of the Copyright, Designs and Patents Act 1988.

ISBN: 978-1-032-11163-6 (hbk)
ISBN: 978-0-367-90307-7 (pbk)
ISBN: 978-1-003-02368-5 (ebk)

DOI: 10.1201/9781003023685

Typeset in Adobe Caslon
by SPi Technologies India Pvt Ltd (Straive)

This book is dedicated to my Lord and Savior, Jesus Christ. It is also dedicated in loving memory to Dr. Gopal Das and Mrs. Kunda Das.

Contents

Acknowledgments

I would like to thank John Wyzalek, my editor, for his help and guidance in the preparation of this book. Many special thanks go out to Bree Ann Russ and Greg Johnson for their contributions to this book as well.

Acknowledgements

I would like to thank [illegible]

Authors

Ravi Das is a business development specialist for The AST Cybersecurity Group, Inc., a leading Cybersecurity content firm located in the Greater Chicago area. Ravi holds a MS in Agribusiness Economics (Thesis in International Trade) and a Master of Business Administration in Management Information Systems.

He has authored seven books, with one more forthcoming on COVID-19 and its impacts on Cybersecurity.

Greg Johnson is the chief executive officer of WebCheck Security, a World Class penetration testing, scanning, and CISO services company. Greg formed Webcheck in early 2018 after a long sales and executive management career with technology companies such as WordPerfect/Novell, SecurityMetrics, Global Access, A-LIGN, and others.

He loves people and providing solutions with integrity. A Brigham Young University graduate, Greg began his technology career in the days of 64k, 5.25" floppy drives and Mac 128k's. As the industry evolved, Greg moved into the cyber arena and learned a great deal about cyber controls, compliance, data breach and response, and in 2016 earned his PCIP or PCI Professional designation.

As former vice president of Business Development with A-LIGN, a multi-national cyber audit and certification firm, Greg consulted, guided, and educated dozens of clients in compliance guidelines and certifications for standards such as:

ISO 2700;
SOC 1 and SOC 2;
GDPR;
FISMA;
FedRAM;
HIPAA;
NIST;
PCI.

Greg also has a thorough grasp on the concepts of web application, infrastructure penetration testing (both internal and external) as well as CISO governance, managed detection and response, incident response and digital forensic investigations. Greg has also co-authored the book entitled *Testing and Securing Web Applications*, and will be co-authoring a future book entitled *Business Recovery and Continuity in a Mega Disaster: Cybersecurity Lessons Learned from the COVID-19 Pandemic*.

Bree Ann Russ is a full-time writer, editor, marketer, and digital specialist with nearly ten years of experience. When she is not writing, she is busy spending time making memories with her family. She and her husband have a total of eight kids between them with a new grandchild on the way, three dogs, and a menagerie of smaller pets. As the matriarch of a large family, Bree Ann Russ loves to create new recipes with her kids and help her husband cook.

CHAPTER 1
CYBERSECURITY RISK

Introduction

There is no doubt that 2020 has been a year of great challenges for the Cybersecurity Industry. The industry had been challenged before, and it was definitely so last year too. But, this level of challenge is expected to grow at a very fast pace given the fact that the COVID-19 pandemic will continue to proliferate at alarming rates, even with new vaccines being approved by the Food and Drug Administration (FDA). New variants of this virus are emerging and they are expected to further proliferate even as still newer ones will arise through mutation and spread themselves to human beings who are the primary host.

There is no doubt that the COVID-19 pandemic has brought an onslaught of new threats as well, some of which have never been seen before. These include the malicious takeover of domains, further exploiting the DNS system, and the total takeover of video conferencing solutions (primarily Zoom, WebEx, Microsoft Teams, Skype, etc.).

Also, the sheer number of phony and fictitious websites has also gone up at an incredible rate, making it even harder for the general public at large to tell what is real and what is fake. It is not just the financial and banking websites that have been at stake, but those of healthcare organizations as well; even the Mom and Pop stores have been replicated with nefarious intent and design.

Phishing attacks have also greatly escalated wherein it is close to impossible to tell what is a real and illegitimate one. Part of this has been due to another phenomenon, which is called "Domain Heisting". Here, the Cyberattacker purchases domains in a bulklike fashion and uses this to cover their tracks. So, while one new domain is created to launch an illegitimate website, another can be used to launch a very sophisticated phishing attack in order to lure unsuspecting victims in an effort to get them to literally "eat the bait". This may lead to the giving away credit card numbers, social security numbers, usernames, passwords, etc.

DOI: 10.1201/9781003023685-1

But, if there is any good that has come out of the COVID-19 pandemic, it has been that of the concept of the Remote Workforce. Of course, working remotely is not a new concept, it has been around for years, but by the sheer gravity and magnitude by which it has taken over the world has been totally unprecedented and even undreamt of. For example, it was forecast that this phenomenon would not happen until the latter part of this century.

But in just a matter of two short months, it really did happen. Of course, in the haste to get workers to work remotely as quickly as possible, many security mistakes were made and many other issues cropped up as well as companies throughout Corporate America so desperately tried hard to deploy corporate issued devices that had the necessary security protocols installed onto them. But even this was not enough, as employees used their own hard wired and wireless devices in order to conduct their daily job tasks.

Another Cybersecurity issue cropped as well. This has been, and will continue to be, the intermingling of the home-based networks of the remote employee along with the corporate networks. As a result, this has left confidential information and data at huge risk for malicious third party interception, as well as the exposure of the Personal Identifiable Information (PII) datasets as they are transmitted across the network mediums and make their way for further processing or storage into the respective database.

The use of Virtual Private Networks (VPNs) has exploded in this regard, and they too are showing their signs of strain of wear and tear. For example, they were designed to handle a Remote Workforce that comprised only about 20%–30% of the employees, and not at the magnitude that is being seen today. As a result, Corporate America is now deploying what is known as the "Next Generation VPN" in order to keep up with the gargantuan increase in demand that has been seen.

Another security issue that has started to emerge with respect to the Remote Workforce has been the sheer inability of the IT Security teams to deploy software patches and upgrades and even firmware upgrades to the devices that the remote employees use every day in order to do their daily tasks.

But despite this, there have been a few other "good areas" that have arisen because of the COVID-19 pandemic. First is the realization of

Corporate America of the sheer need to have Incident Response (IR)/ Disaster Recovery (DR)/Business Continuity (BC) plans in place. For example, it is the IR plan that dictates how an IT Security team responds to a Cyberattack as it is occurring in real time, it is the DR plan that spells out how the IT Security team should bring in mission critical operations and procedures in the shortest time frame possible (such as within hours), and it is the BC plan that also guides the IT Security team on how to bring back the business for a long term after it has been impacted.

In this regard, it is the BC plan that is probably one of the most crucial pieces of documentation that needs to be compiled. For example, this will address how a corporation should approach the indirect costs, which include brand damage, reputational loss, and lost customers, coming into compliance with the likes of the CCPA and the GDPR (these will be much further explored in Chapter 4 of this book), setting civil- and criminal-based lawsuits, etc.

Another good aspect that has come out of the COVID-19 pandemic has been the realization by Corporate America of the need to fully adopt a Cloud-based Platform, such as that of the Amazon Web Services (AWS) or Microsoft Azure. In this regard, a company can take their entire On Premises IT and Network Infrastructures into the Cloud, which offers a whole package of advantages. One of them is that the Remote Workforce can now access all of the digital assets and shared resources that they need anytime and from anywhere that they may be in the world, in a safe and secure fashion that no On Premises IT and Network Infrastructure could ever afford to them.

But in the end, it all comes down to just one thing which is at stake for the Corporate as a whole: gauging their levels of Cyber Risk and the associated tolerance level. Loosely put, this translates to the fact as to what level of uncertainty a particular business can tolerate before the issue starts to have a serious impact upon their mission critical flows and processes.

Trying to gauge this can be a very huge and nebulous task for any IT Security team to accomplish. For example, there are many frameworks and models that can be utilized, and it can be very confusing to anybody as to which one to utilize in order to achieve high level of security for their organization. Complicating this fact is that both quantitative and qualitative variables have to be taken into consideration and deployed into the Cyber Risk model.

Therefore, the goal of this book is to provide a much greater insight into how to gauge your particular level of Cyber Risk and what will be deemed to be appropriate for your company or corporation. But keep in mind that it is not just the level of Cyber Risk that you have to compute. You also need to determine the appropriate controls that are needed to implement them, as well as the standards and best practices that your IT Security needs to set in place into comply with the regulations and mandates of the CCPA, GDPR, HIPAA, etc. For better readability, this book will be divided into the following chapters:

Chapter 1: Understanding the Mechanics of Cyber Risk;
Chapter 2: The Controls That Need to Be Put into Place;
Chapter 3: The Issues and Benefits of Cybersecurity Risk Insurance Policies;
Chapter 4: A Deep Dive into The GDPR, CCPA, and the CMMC;
Chapter 5: Conclusions.

In this chapter, we first start off with the concept of what Measurement is all about, as this is probably the biggest starting point when it comes to calculating and gauging Cyber Risk.

What Cyber Measurement Is All About

If you were to ask a CISO or an IT Security team lead what the concept of Measurement is, you would get all sorts of answers. From the C-Suite, it will be about all of the costs and the impacts to the bottom line, and to the more technical crowd, a whole slew of metrics would crop up, ranging from how long it would take to detect a threat variant from penetrating into the IT and Network Infrastructure of a business to how long it would take to mitigate it.

But the key thing to be remembered is that before any sort of Cyber Risk can be gauged, it must first be measured somehow, whether quantitatively or qualitatively, in units that are suitable for the environment that it is associated with. But is this something that can be calculated by making use of a ruler or a clock? Perhaps it could be, but a much more sound, technical definition for Cyber Risk mitigation can be given as follows:

A quantitatively expressed reduction of uncertainty based on one or more observations.[1]

The given definition obviously differs greatly from the traditional text-based ones because in the world of Cybersecurity, Cyber Risk mitigation applies primarily to the exposure of threat variants and how they can be reduced both in the short term and the long term. The level and type of controls that will be needed will largely be dependent on these observations once they have been ascertained by the IT Security team. In fact, this foundation for Measurement, as it relates to Cybersecurity, goes all the way back to a scientific paper that was published by an American mathematician, Claude Shannon. It was entitled "A Mathematical Theory of Communications", published all the way back in 1940.

So as you can see, this concept of Measurement goes back in time by well over 60 years, and it even relates to the world of Information Technology in general. In fact, his definition of uncertainty relies upon the concepts of electrical engineering, in which the effects of the amplifications of various signals from the circuit board could be almost eradicated through the use of what is known as "Entropy".

Now comes the issue of units that have to be tagged along with the concept of Measurement. To the CISO and the IT Security team, the common notion here is to create a series of categories, and from there, establish a categorical scale, perhaps ranging from 1 to 10, where 1 would indicate the least amount of Cyber Risk and 10 would pose the greatest amount of Cyber Risk. But as it relates to Cybersecurity, a special exception can be made here. While the level of uncertainty has to be mathematically expressed in some way or fashion (such as the categorical scale just described), what is actually being observed does not have to be quantitative per se.

For example, as was mentioned earlier in the BC plan, the indirect costs, which must be recovered after the organization has been impacted by a Cyberattack, were well focused on. The cost of lost customers and the cost of procuring new ones are some of the examples.

Now while the actual topic of Measurement is much more qualitative in nature, the cost that must be presented in the CISO and to his or her Board of Directors must be quantified in terms of dollars and cents.

It can be seen in the world of Cybersecurity that it is typically the Nominal and Ordinal scales that are used the most. The former scales are probably more applicable to events that are more qualitative in nature, whereas the latter scales are most appropriate for those events in Cybersecurity which need to be assigned some sort of number. But the issue here is that there is no level of order of magnitude to the numerical scores that are calculated and reported.

But it is very important to note as to how the Nominal and Ordinal scales will be applied to the kind of Cyber environment and what their long term usage will be. The Cybersecurity Threat Landscape is a forever changing one. In this regard, the establishment of labels relating to the unit of these Nominal and Ordinal scales also becomes very important. For example, the labels that are given subsequently are most relevant in certain conditions:

- The Annual Probability of a Cyber Event Occurring;
- The Statistical Distribution of Potential Losses.

The Concept of Bayesian Measurement

So far, we have reviewed the concept of Measurement just from the standpoint of a definition. Whether the data that is being collected, processed, and examined is quantitative or qualitative in nature, it is very important to note here that the bottom line of any type of analyses that take place in the world of Cybersecurity always makes use of rather high level, sophisticated statistics. In fact, the biggest buzzwords that are being bandied about right now are that of Artificial Intelligence (AI) and Machine Learning (ML).

While these technologies sound ultra-sophisticated due to the names given to them, it is important to note that the models they use are simple statistical-based ones. They merely take in data and give the output in the format of an expected outcome. This is also known as merely "Garbage In and Garbage Out". So when we refer to such things as reducing the level of uncertainty, the concept of

"Probability" often comes into play. For example, most of the metrics and the Key Performance Indicators (KPIs) that are associated with them have relevant Probability levels, such as whether a particular event is going to happen or not and if and when it would occur.

This whole notion of putting most things in the realm of statistical probabilities comes from the world of what is known as "Bayesian Statistics". Thomas Bayes is the actual founder of this scientific pillar, going back all the way to the 18th century. He invented what is known as "Bayes Theorem". The underlying crux of this new information/data can be updated by using past events, also known as the "levels of Probability". So for example, if there has been an existing phishing threat vector, any new variants that come out of it can be assigned a new level of Probability of occurring. In other words, Phishing Attack X occurred, then you could say that Phishing X.1 has a likelihood of 98% of occurring. You are taking past attack signatures to formulate a scientific hypothesis as to what the future could potentially hold. But it is also important to keep in mind here as well that not all probabilities are subject to just past events which are made up of raw data.

It can also incorporate certain levels of personal beliefs as well, such as a malware researcher making use of his or her insight and intuition in order to figure when a malicious act be potentially deployed over a certain period of time. Also, statistical-based Probabilities do not have to measure or gauge something that is going to happen in the future; they can also reflect the possibilities of something happening at this point of time as well. Finally, there is no such thing as reducing uncertainty to a level that is mathematically zero. In theory this may be possible, but not in the real world of Cybersecurity. As long as there is some recognizable decrease in uncertainty, that is all that matters in the end.

The Classification Chain

So now the question arises as to what the exact process is that is involved when trying to associate a past event with a future event when a level of Probability is attached to it (such as in our previous phishing example). There is a term for this, and it is technically known as the "Classification Chain". It can be defined as follows:

Step 1: "If it matters at all, it is then detectable and/or observable.
Step 2: If it is indeed detectable, it can then be further detected by using an amount (or a range of possible amounts).
Step 3: If it can be detected as a range of possible amounts, it can then be measured".[1]

In other words, for the sake of an example, the malware researcher is considering something that has happened in the past, making use of qualitative assumptions and inferences. This can be deemed to be intangible in nature, because there are no quantitative measures that are associated with it. He or she is now considering all of this to help predict a future event, which is now thus tangible, because it has a probability of occurrence that is associated with it. One of the primary goals of the Classification Chain is to further ascertain what is known as an "Object of Measurement", which in this case would be the newer phishing threat variant that is going to be launched in the future.

There are also other concepts that are associated with Measurement and statistical Probabilities, which can be used now to expand quantifying further as to how something can happen in the future or the reduction of the likelihood of it from actually happening at all. These new terms can be defined as follows:

Uncertainty

This is the sheer lack of complete certainty that is the existence of more than one possibility. The "true" outcome/state/result/value is not known.

Measurement of Uncertainty

This is a set of probabilities assigned to a set of possibilities.

Risk

"This is the state of uncertainty where some possibilities involve a loss, catastrophe, or other undesirable outcome".

Measurement of Risk

The set of possibilities, each with quantified probabilities and quantified losses.[1]

Let's break these definitions down a bit further for clarification. Suppose you have undeniable faith and evidence that something will happen. This can be referred to also technically as "100% Certainty". But what if some new information comes about that casts some doubt into your mind about this? This is where a level of unsureness will then set in. Now that you are convinced that some other events are possible, you want to know for sure to what degree that they could occur, and this is where the assignment of Probabilities then comes into play. These are the "Measurements of Uncertainty".

Now that you know what the other possibilities are, and the chances of them occurring in the real world, you want to know to the level of degree that the damage will be. In the world of Cybersecurity, this can be viewed as a piece of malware that can be used to determine the level of probability that it will be hit in order to exfiltrate the usernames and passwords that are stored in those databases. It is important to keep in mind here that the term "risk" very often has a negative hypothesis that is associated with it. But there is flip side to this as well, which is the positive outcome. For example, if you deploy a certain control in your IT and Network Infrastructure, what is the risk of malware not hitting upon the digital asset that it is serving to protect? Finally, once you know what the risk is that your company is facing, you then want to quantify it to some degree or another, which is using some sort of Measurement scale based on the theories of statistics. A good example of this is what is known as the "coefficients of variation".

It can be technically defined as follows:

A coefficient of variation (CV) can be calculated and interpreted in two different settings: analyzing a single variable and interpreting a model. The standard formulation of the CV, the ratio of the standard deviation to the mean, applies in the single variable setting. In the modeling setting, the CV is calculated as the ratio of the root mean squared error

(RMSE) to the mean of the dependent variable. In both settings, the CV is often presented as the given ratio multiplied by 100. The CV for a single variable aims to describe the dispersion of the variable in a way that does not depend on the variable's Measurement unit. The higher the CV, the greater the dispersion in the variable. The CV for a model aims to describe the model fit in terms of the relative sizes of the squared residuals and outcome values. The lower the CV, the smaller the residuals relative to the predicted value. This is suggestive of a good model fit.[2]

In other words, the coefficient of variation is merely a statistical ratio of the Standard Deviation that is correlated to its Mean. It is normally expressed as a percentage. If this level is high, it means that there is a greater dispersion around the mean, and thus, the level of risk cannot be ascertained with much certainty. So, the rule of thumb here is that you want this particular percentage to be as low as possible so that the confidence in the level of risk that has been computed remains much higher.

The Statistical Methods of Measurement

Very often in the world of Cybersecurity, especially as it relates it to statistics, you will hear researchers talk about what is known as "Statistical Significance". Just what does it exactly mean? A technical definition of it is as follows:

> Statistical significance is the likelihood that a relationship between two or more variables in an analysis is not purely coincidental, but is actually caused by another factor. In other words, statistical significance is a way of mathematically proving that a certain statistic is reliable.[3]

As it can be related to Cybersecurity, this simply means that two or more events which can lead to the hypothesis of an actual threat variant from occurring is for real, and is not impacted by any other factors. So in other words, if you get two or more pieces of data that are statistically significant, you can be reasonably sure that the predictive powers they possess have some real meaning to them, and should thus be taken seriously when trying to predict what the Cybersecurity Threat Landscape could potentially look like in the future.

Here some myths about Statistical Significance that are debunked:

- There is no predefined sample size that is required to yield a "Statistically Significant" result;
- In order to make the level of Statistical Significance as real as possible, it must also be associated with a variance of the sample size that is being examined and the Null Hypothesis that is being tested. This is all factored together and is known technically as the "P-Value". This is then compared to a pre-computed "Level of Significance".
- You can actually get a good measure by simply using a very small random sample from a very large sample population set.
- You can still get a good Measurement Level even when many other unknown variables are present in the sample size. Actually for Cybersecurity, this is a good point because the Threat Landscape is always changing on a dynamic basis, and thus, there are many new unknowns or uncertainties that come into play.
- You can also get a good Measurement Level of rare events that could occur in the future. A good example of this so far which fortunately has not happened is a cataclysmic shutdown of all Critical Infrastructure due to a massive Cyberattack. This would include the water supply, food supply, gas and oil lines, the national power grid, etc.

The Rule of Five

In the world of statistics, you must have a sample of at least five different observations in order to have any form of Statistical Significance to be associated with it. This particular sample size can be literally five of anything. This has become known as the "Rule of Five", and it can be described as follows:

There is a 93.75% statistical chance that the median of the sample size being observed and studied will be at 50%. In other words, what are the chances that the Median of the sample size is half below and half above of the largest and smallest numerical values in the data set that is being examined.

The Various Quantitative Methods for Gauging Cyber Risk

In this part of the chapter, we will introduce some simpler forms on how the CISO and their IT Security team can start to compute the particular level of Cyber Risk that their company is exposed to on a daily basis. We first start off with what is known as the "Risk Matrix".

The Risk Matrix

If one were to conduct a Google search and correlate that with Cybersecurity, there are many forms of Risk Matrices that one can use. The one we will examine in some more detail here is known as the "Substitution Method". In this situation, the attempt is made to get rid of just employing mathematical-based Absolute Values, which are based on a categorical scale, such as 1–5 or 1–10. While it is important to have these, the primary objective here is to associate some sort of finite Statistical Probabilities to go with them.

The following matrix exemplifies this:

THE STATEMENT	THE SUBSTITUTION
"The Rating likelihood on a scale of 1 to 5 or 'low to high'".	"Estimating the probability of the event occurring in a given period of time".
"The Rating Impact on a scale of 1 to 5 or 'low to high'".	"Estimating a 90% confidence interval for a monetized loss".
"Plotting likelihood and impact scores on a Risk Matrix".	"Using the quantitative likelihood and impact to generate a 'low exceedance curve' – a quantitative approach to expressing Risk. This can be done using simple Monte Carlo methods".
"Further dividing the Risk Matrix into Risk Categories like Low/Medium/High".	"Comparing the loss exceedance curve to a Risk tolerance curve and prioritizing actions based upon return on mitigation".

Source: "How to Measure Anything In Cybersecurity Risk". Daniel Geer and Stuart McClure. John Wiley and Sons, 2016.

Thus, a very simple Risk Matrix can thus be constructed by incorporating the following steps:

1) Define the list of Cyber Risks that your company is facing based on expert opinion from the CISO and members on the IT Security team.
2) Clearly define the specific time period over which a particular event could be happening. For example, Threat Variant X happening from February 2021 to April 2021.

3) For each Cyber Risk that has been identified, assign a random probability for it actually happening. Note that this will not be an actual computed value, but rather it will be subjective in nature based upon expert opinion. For example, "A data breach will occur for application X in the next 12 months".[1]

4) For each level of Cyber Risk that has been identified, assign a best estimated monetary value to it. For example, "If there is a data breach of application X, then it is 90% likely that there will be a loss equal to somewhere between $1 Million and $10 Million".[1]

5) From within the CISO and the members of your IT Security team, try to get different expert opinions, from them individually and not as a group. The primary purpose of this is to decrease the level biasness as much as possible, while at the same time, proportionately increasing the levels of impartiality at the same time.

In the world of Cybersecurity, there are often misgivings about using expert opinion as a key Measurement tool. But, these data points, although they may be qualitative in nature, are still much needed when you are first building your Cyber Risk Matrix into becoming a detailed, much more comprehensive one as time goes on. Just remember this key saying whenever you have doubts about using expert opinion in this regard:

> Remember, if the primary concern about using probabilistic methods is the lack of data, then you also lack the data to use non quantitative methods.[1]

The Monte Carlo Method

It is important to keep in mind that when using expert opinion, there could very likely be a set of ranges that the CISO and their IT Security may have to deal with. So now this further brings up the question of how can you predict with some level of certainty that a Cybersecurity event will most likely happen in the near future? This is where the Monte Carlo method comes into play. With this statistical concept, one create a large number of "What If" based scenarios based upon a range of statistical probabilities. For every Cybersecurity event that you want to predict, a specific statistical value can thus be generated for all of the unknown variables that have not been accounted for.

Typically, Excel-based spreadsheets can be used to help adopt the usage of the Monte Carlo techniques when it comes to predicting new threat variants and the likelihood of them actually happening in the near future. But keep in mind that spreadsheets do have their limitations, and trying to create extremely sophisticated Monte Carlo methods will need the reliance of both AI and ML tools, both of which are out of the scope of this book to cover. Instead, we will closely examine how to implement simple Monte Carlo simulations into the Excel spreadsheet.

The Creation of Random Cyber–Related Events
To compute a single risk value for just one kind of Cyber-related event, you can randomly generate a numerical value of "1" if the event actually does happen, and a numerical value of "0" if it actually does not happen at all. Also, the value of "1" will be mathematically equal to the stated probability of the Cyber-related event actually occurring. The formula for doing this in Excel is as follows:

$$= \text{if}\left[\left(rand() < \text{event\_probability}, 1, 0\right)\right]$$

So, if the Event Probability is .125, then the above equation should yield a value which produces the numerical value of "1". This simply translates to the fact that the Cyber-related event has actually occurred somewhere, at some subsequent point in time. Now while the above equation will tell of an actual event has transpired or not, you also need to know what kind of impact it will bring to the company. This can be done by using the "Inverse Probability Function" that is also available in Excel. This demonstrated by the following mathematical formula:

$$= \text{norminv}\left(\text{probability,mean,standard deviation}\right)$$

One statistical-based concept that has not been reviewed so far in this chapter is that of the "Standard Deviation". It can be technically defined as follows:

> The standard deviation is a statistic that measures the dispersion of a dataset relative to its mean and is calculated as the square root of the variance. The standard deviation is calculated as the square root of variance by determining each data point's deviation relative to the mean. If the data points are further from the mean, there is a higher deviation within the data set; thus, the more spread out the data, the higher the standard deviation.[4]

It can be calculated from the following mathematical formula:

$$O = \text{SQUARE ROOT} \left[\Sigma (Xi - U)^{\wedge} 2 \right] / N$$

where
O = The population Standard Deviation;
N = The size of the population;
Xi = Each value from the population;
N = The population mean.

The Standard Deviation can very often be used to compute calculate the statistical-based upper bounds and lower bounds for estimating a range of possible losses in the event of a Cybersecurity attack, should it occur.

The Lognormal Distribution

While making use of the Standard Deviation can provide a range of possible losses, a much accurate picture of it can be gained by making use of what are known as "Lognormal Distributions". This can be technically defined as follows:

> A lognormal (log-normal or Galton) distribution is a probability distribution with a normally distributed logarithm. A random variable is log normally distributed if its logarithm is normally distributed.[5]

The Lognormal Distribution is also referred to more commonly as the "Bell Shaped Curve". But in many cases, the curve can very often be skewed to either the left or right of the graph, and this actually represents large amounts of data loss, and as it applies to the world of Cybersecurity, this would be the total Dollar loss after a Cybersecurity attack has occurred.

To create a Lognormal Distribution in Excel, use the following mathematical formula:

$$= \text{lognorm.inv}\left(rand\,(\,), \text{Mean of }\left(\ln(X)\right), \\ \text{Standard Deviation of }\left(\ln(X)\right)\right)$$

where

The Standard Deviation of ln(X) = (lnUB) − ln(LB)) /3.29;
Mean of ln(X) = (ln(UB) + ln(LB))/2)

As an example, if you want to calculate a Cybersecurity event happening at a 5% Confidence Interval, which has a potential Dollar loss in the range of $1 million to $9 million, you would use the following mathematical formula in Excel:

$$\text{If}\left(rand(\,) < .05, \text{lognorm.inv}\left(rand(\,), \left(\ln(9000000000) + \ln(1000000000)\right)/2, \\ \left(\ln(9000000000) + \ln(1000000000)\right)/3.29\right), 0\right)$$

One note of caution of making use Lognormal Distributions is that both the upper bounds (UB) and lower bounds (LB) of the statistical curve can be mistaken for extreme losses, which in most cases that really may not be the case. So in other words, there is a subjective component to it, which also needs to be taken into consideration.

The Summation of the Cyber Risks

All of the variables we have discussed so far in this section can be summed into one table. The primary advantage of this is that this can be presentable in an easy-to-read format for both the C-Suite and the Board of Directors. With it being comprehensible at a quick glance, the chances of getting more financial Dollars for already crimped Cybersecurity Budgets will be even stronger for next budget request. Here is an example of such a table, as illustrated below:

Table 1.1 The Probability of Getting An Increased Funding for The Cyber Budget

EVENT	PROBABILITY OF EVENT HAPPENING IN A YEAR	LOWER BOUND OF 90% CI	UPPER BOUND OF 90% CI	THE RANDOM RESULT
AA	.1	$50,000.00	$500,000	0
AB	.05	$100,000.00	$10,000,000.00	$8,456,193
AC	.01	$200,000.00	$25,000,000.00	0
AD	.03	$100,000.00	$15,000,000.00	0
AE	.05	$250,000.00	$30,000,000.00	0
AF	.1	$200,000.00	$2,000,000.00	0
AG	.07	$1,000,000.00	$10,000,000.00	$2,111,284
AH	.02	$100,000.00	$15,000,000.00	0
ZM	.05	$250,000.00	$30,000,000.00	0
ZN	.01	$1,500,000.00	$40,000,000.00	0
Total Amount of Losses:				$23,345,193.00

Source: "How to Measure Anything In Cybersecurity Risk". Daniel Geer and Stuart McClure. John Wiley and Sons, 2016.

This is a sort of table that can be easily created in an Excel spreadsheet by making specific use of the "Data Table" and "What If Analysis" functionalities that are embedded from within it. With this kind of table, you can create as many Cyber-related scenarios as you need, depending upon your requirements. But when running all of your "What If Scenarios", keep in mind that one of the most important is possibly those Cyber events that are deemed to be rare, but have the most impact in terms of Dollar Loss. In fact, by using the Table 1.1 and creating in Excel, you are technically running Monte Carlo-based Cyber-related scenarios.

How to Visualize Cyber Losses

Up to this point in this chapter, we have presented nothing but absolute, mathematical-based Numerical Values, and various sorts of Cyber Risk Tables and Matrices. We have now come up to the point where all of this needs to be visually plotted in order to reinforce the gravity, meaning, and the sheer magnitude of the numbers that are being presented. This is technically known as the "Loss Exceedance Curve", or the "LEC" for short. In this scenario, the vertical (or Y-Axis) can be represented with just a single point in time, or even multiple ones, if necessary. But instead of a Numerical Score, it will be replaced with various the various Statistical Probabilities that have been calculated. The horizontal axis (or the X-axis) will of course be the Dollar amount of loss that is expected to occur given each degree of Statistical Probability that is depicted on the Y-Axis.

In addition to the Loss Exceedance Curve, there are also three others curves that can be plotted against as well, and these are as follows:

- The Inherent Risk Curve (IRC);
- The Residual Risk Curve (RRC);
- The Risk Tolerance Curve (RTC).

The IRC represents the particular level of risk that a company is exposed to before the controls are put in place in order to further reduce that level of risk; the RRC represents the risk that still remains or lingers after the implementation of the controls; and the RTC demonstrates the level of risk the company can tolerate without experiencing any severe repercussions both in the short term and the long term. It is important to note at this point that if the IRC is visually above the RTC, then claims can be made that the company cannot tolerate this certain level of risk, because the RTC curve is then deemed to be statistically "broken".

But if the RTC Curve is below the RTC, the risk can then deemed to be rather negligible, because the RTC technically "stochastically dominates" the RRC. In other words, this particular level of Cyber Risk is deemed to be acceptable to the company in question.

Also, the Loss Exceedance Curve can be exhibited via a Statistical Histogram, which is exemplified below:

THE TOTAL AMOUNT OF DOLLAR LOSS	THE PROBABILITY PER YEAR OF LOSS OR GREATER
No Dollar Loss	99.9%
$500,000.00	98.8%
$1,000,000.00	95.8%
$1,500,000.00	92.8%
$200,000,000.00	86.4%
$2,500,000.00	83.4%
$300,000,000.00	77.5%
$24,000,000.00	3.0%
$24,500,000.00	2.7%

Source: "How to Measure Anything In Cybersecurity Risk". Daniel Geer and Stuart McClure. John Wiley and Sons, 2016.

The first column clearly indicates the series of losses that are possible, based on Dollar amounts. The second column shows the percentage of those losses in actually occurring, based upon the Monte Carlo methods. If you need to create this in Excel, then the most basic command that you would use in this particular instance is that of the "Countif()" functionality. The specific formula for achieving this task is as follows:

$$= \text{Countif} \left(\text{Monte Carlo Results, ">" \& Loss} \right) / 10,000.00$$

This functionality that is available in Excel literally counts the number of Statistical Values in the predefined range that meets a certain type of Cyber-related event.

Although the LEC Curve can prove to be very advantageous, it does have its fair share of limitations as well. For example, if they are too many of them that are displayed on one graph, it can get to look quite confusing. But this of course is highly dependent upon how big the datasets are that you are making use of. But, there are two ways around this:

- You can create separate LEC Plots for each separate category;
- You can have aggregate LEC Plots where LEC Curve can be displayed onto a separate, detailed chart for that specific LEC Curve that is currently being examined.

The Return on Mitigation

It is important to keep in mind that the primary objective of all of the concepts and principles laid out this far in this chapter is to ultimately support the decision-making process of the CISO and their IT Security Managers when it comes to mitigating, or further reducing the levels of Cyber Risk that they are currently experiencing, or that they could potentially face down the road. The bottom line is that it all comes down to the determining the proper levels of Resource Allocation, an area which has not been clearly addressed yet. So in order to do this, it is thus important to include yet another calculation that the CISO and their team can use readily, and this is known as the "Return on Mitigation". It can be also referred to at times as the "Return on Control".

The mathematical formula for doing this is demonstrated below:

$$\text{Return on Control} = \left(\text{Return in Expected Losses} / \text{Cost of Control}\right) - 1$$

The term "Expected Loss" merely refers to the amount of a Monte Carlo-based Simulation Loss based upon some sort of negative event that can happen, such as that of a Cyberattack. In other words, this is also the Statistical Weighted Average of some level of probability of the amount of loss that is triggered by a particular event. This formula also represents the mathematical difference of a monetary loss in the event that a Cyberattack were to occur, before the controls were implemented and after the controls were implemented to avoid this type of threat variant from occurring in the future at some subsequent point in time.

A few key points need to be mentioned here about the Return on Control:

- If the Return in Expected Losses were equal to the Cost of the Control that is to be implemented, then the resultant would be merely a flat out "0".
- You need to clearly identify what the specific time period is when the expected Return in Expected Losses were to actually occur.
- The Return on Control can be used only for one specific time period making use of just one Cyber-related event. If the need ever arises where the CISO and the IT Security team need to decompose this particular formula for multiple Cyber-related events that make use of multiple variables or components, then the formula can greatly lose its effectiveness for showing how well a particular Control is working. In other words, if you need to use this formula, separate Monte Carlo simulations then need to be run for all of the Cyber-related events that are currently being examined.

The Decomposition of the One for One Substitution Cyber Risk Model

So far in this chapter, with all of the models and variables that we have presented so far, only the major categories that should be incorporated have been included. While this can serve as a great framework for getting an idea of your initial level of Cyber Risk, the only way to gauge the real picture is by including the other subvariables or other subcategories into your decision-making process.

For example, when you calculate the loss after you have been hit by a major Cybersecurity attack, there are a lot of factors that go into calculating the indirect costs. It is not so easy to calculate the direct costs, as these will primarily be just Numerical-based values. For example, in this realm of indirect costs, here are some of the other subcategories that you will need to consider as well:

- The costs of brand/reputational damage;
- The costs of losing customers;
- The costs of trying to gain lost customers back;
- The costs of trying to appease lost and potentially lost customers, which include the following:
  - The costs of issuing free credit reports;
  - The costs of keeping them appraised of what is going on (especially if you make use of "Snail Mail");
  - The costs of any lawsuits that you could be facing;
  - Etc.
- Any legal costs that are associated in case you are audited by GDPR and/or CCPA regulators/auditors;
- Any financial penalties that you may have to pay as a result if one of the causes of the security breach has been deemed to as a result of noncompliance with any of these two legislations;
- Etc.

The above list should give you a good idea of what would need to be further decomposed. But keep in mind that this list does not end there; the mentioned categories will have their own levels of subcategories as well. So, where can one start in this regard? Probably the best way to do this is to get started with what is known as the "CIA Model". This is a particular framework that can be broken down as follows:

1) Confidentiality
   This refers to keeping mission critical information and data (such as PII datasets) safe and secure, and away from the hands of malicious third parties;

2) Integrity

This refers to the scenario wherein any mission critical information and data that is transmitted back and forth remains intact and has not been altered by any means. The term transmission is often referred to as messages and/or communication that are sent back and forth between the sending and receiving parties, and vice versa.

3) Availability

The mission critical information and data will always be available (with at least a guaranteed uptime of 99.999%) in the case of any breach, whether it is intentional or not, physical, or virtual.

By making use of the CIA model, just about any type or kind of Cyber-related event can be broken down or "decomposed" into its constituent parts. But the key here is to define firmly and without any sort of ambiguity what that event was. From there, you can then further determine which parts of the CIA model have been particularly impacted. You can then create a table with any of the major components of the CIA model that have been impacted. Table 1.2 is a clear demonstration of this.

Table 1.2 The Impacts To The CIA Model

EVENT	PROBABILITY OF OCCURRENCE	CONFIDENTIALITY	AVAILABILITY	BOTH TYPES
AA	.1	.2	.7	.1
AB	.05	.3	.5	.2
AC	.01	.1	.8	.1
AD	.03	0	0	1.0
AE	.05	0	.8	.4

Source: "How to Measure Anything In Cybersecurity Risk". Daniel Geer and Stuart McClure. John Wiley and Sons, 2016.

EVENT	CI – LOWER BOUND	CI – UPPER BOUND OUTAGE (HOURS)	CI – UB	CI – LOWER BOUND
AA	$50.00	$50.00	.25	4
AB	$100.00	$10,000.00	.25	8
AC	$200.00	$25,000.00	.25	12
AD	$100.00	$15,000.00	.25	2
AE	$250.00	$30,000.00	1	24

Source: "How to Measure Anything In Cybersecurity Risk". Daniel Geer and Stuart McClure. John Wiley and Sons, 2016.

Notes:

UB = Upper Bound of Outage, represented in hours
This is a continuation of the Table 1.2.

EVENT	LOWER BOUND – COST/HOUR	UPPER BOUND – COST/HOUR
AA	$2.00	$10.00
AB	$1.00	$10.00
AC	$40.00	$200.00
AD	$2.00	$10.00
AE	$5.00	$50.00

Source: "How to Measure Anything In Cybersecurity Risk". Daniel Geer and Stuart McClure. John Wiley and Sons, 2016.

Tables 1.2 show how you can further decompose the CIA Model in terms of outage (which can also be translated into Downtime) and the Cost per Hour. Note that the above Decomposed Variables only further impact the Confidentiality and Availability aspects of the CIA Model. Also, Tables 1.2 can be put into Excel by making use of the following mathematical formula:

$$= \text{If}\left(rand() < \text{ConfInt}, 1 \, \text{if} \left(rand() < \text{ConfInt} + \text{Avail}, 2, 3 \right) \right)$$

It is important to note at this point that these two aspects, namely the Availability and Confidentiality, could also have been examined separately. But for purposes of presentation to both the C-Suite and the Board of Directors, it is always prudent to have everything presented as much as possible in one table. With regards to the financial losses when it comes to Availability, this can be computed as follows:

$$\text{Hours of Outage} * \text{Cost Per Hour}$$

Also, the financial losses can be computed for Confidentiality in the same manner, by using the very same mathematical formula. But keep in mind here that Confidentiality can have two meanings of reference. For example, once the confidential information and data (such as the PII datasets) have been restored by the IT Security team into the newly created databases that have been impacted, it is deemed to be that the Confidentiality of the datasets have been restored. Second, it is also very important to keep in mind that when breached information or data that has fallen into the hands of a malicious third party, it is no longer deemed to be confidential by nature. The only way this status can change is when the impacted parties involved (such as the customers and the employees) have been notified and corrective actions have been taken in order to establish new datasets (such as getting a new credit card number, Social Security number, bank account, etc.).

A Decomposition Strategy

It should be noted here that all of the events described so far in this chapter have been Cyber-related events. So in this regard, one way to decompose the aspects of the CIA Model is to think of the applications as well as the events that have triggered them. Here, you are actually further breaking down the events into the applications that have been impacted by them.

This is illustrated in below:

Some examples of Application Decompositions are shown in Table 1.3.

It is important to note that Table 1.3 is not an exhaustive list by any means. There are other events and their impacts to applications that could take place as well. In the next subsection, we take a closer look as to how you can further refine or define the events and the sub applications below them in the event of a Cybersecurity breach.

Table 1.3 The Cyber Impacts to the CIA Model

APPLICATION	DESCRIPTION
Financial Theft	Credit card numbers, banking savings, and checking account numbers
System Outages	How any downtime affects the following: • The total number of end users involved; • The financial loss experienced by the impacted departments, such as that of sales
Investigation/ Remediation Costs	How any downtime affects the following: • How long does it take to fix or restore the impacted systems; • How many people are needed for the restoration process; • The hourly costs that are involved in order to launch and complete the Restoration Process
Intellectual Property	This can include trade secrets, patents, trademarks, etc.
Notification/Credit Monitoring	Paying for Notification and Credit Monitoring Services to impacted customers and employees
Legal Liabilities and Fines	The costs for not coming into regulatory compliance with the GDPR, CCPA, and HIPAA
Other Types of Interference	The costs of security breaches associated with external, third party vendors
Reputation	This is primarily financial losses that are associated with damaged brand and image from the result of a Cyberattack

Source: "How to Measure Anything In Cybersecurity Risk". Daniel Geer and Stuart McClure. John Wiley and Sons, 2016.

A Newer Decomposition Strategy

So far, we have reviewed the principles of Decomposition. But at this point, it is very important to note that there are no sets of practices or best standards governing this concept. This means what one CISO and his/her IT Security team calculates as losses or risks could be entirely different from that of another CISO and their IT Security team. Keep in mind also that every Cybersecurity company has their own area of practice, expertise, and specializations. The end result is the variables that are used to calculate risk and loss to one Cybersecurity company may have no relevance to another one.

The reason for this is that some businesses could be literally virtual, so the downtime that is experienced could be much less. But for those Cyber-related businesses that still maintain a traditional brick and mortar presence, the costs could be much greater. So in this subsection, we further evaluate a new list of variables that can not only cut across all scopes of Cybersecurity, but for just about any type or kind of industry that is not even Cyber related.

Thus, here is an entirely new set of Cyber-related Decomposition variables that the CISO and their IT Security team should take a closer look at when attempting to calculate Cyber Risk and Loss.

1) Clearness/Conciseness

This is probably one of the biggest problems that is facing the Cybersecurity Industry today. So, in order to resolve it, the CISO and their IT Security team need to formulate, establish, and deploy a line of communications that is extremely crystal clear, so everybody knows what they are talking about and are thus on the same page. This typically starts from the top, with the C-Suite (especially the CISO), and cascades downward to all employees in the end, not just the IT Security team.

2) Observable

Whatever subvariables are being used to calculate the Cyber Risk and Losses must somehow be observable to all members of the IT Security team. For example, if the company was hit with a malware attack, just where was the impact? Are there are signature profiles that have been created so that it can be tracked into the future as well? In order to make things much more observable as well as coherent to all of those that are involved, making use of both AI and ML tools can greatly help in this regard, as they can serve as a repository for storing these attack signatures and further analyzing them in real time.

3) Usefulness

In order to create a common set of standards that each and every CISO and IT Security team can use, the Decomposed Variables that are used to calculate the level of Cyber Risk and Losses must have some meaning behind them (whether it is quantitative or qualitative), so that they would prove to be "useful" across all grounds. In other words, the Decomposed Variables must be able to aid in the decision-making process.

How to Avoid Over-Decomposing the Variables

Further Decomposing the variables are presented to the CISO and their IT Security team is technically known as "Informative Decomposition". In other words, you have done as much breaking down of the variables as much as you could while making them effective for calculating the level of Cyber Risk and Losses that could be present. But, it is quite possible that while trying to impress the Board of Directors, the CISO and their IT Security team could go into even further detail, thus eradicating altogether the purpose of decomposing the variables. This now becomes technically known as "Informative Decomposition", because the value of what you are attempting to calculate will soon start to lose its value to it, just due to the sheer amount of statistical-based "Noise Level" that is now involved with it.

In other words, the CISO and the IT Security team are now making use of concepts that they are more familiar with and that may not resonate as well with others, especially if there is a certain level of cross-collaboration involved in order to combat a certain threat variant. In other words, "Over-Decomposing" (as it is also called) and creating purely abstract values could hold some meaning in theory, but in reality, they do not.

Table 1.4 summarizes some of the most important rules when applying the Decomposition process.

Table 1.4 The Components of the Statistical Decomposition Rules

DECOMPOSITION RULE NUMBER	THE DECOMPOSITION RULE
#1	Only Decompose those variables that you are familiar with, or can obtain the data for, whether it is quantitative or qualitative
#2	Confirm the Statistical Validity of your Decomposed Variables with a simulation test, that can be done in excel, with the formulas provided in the chapter
#3	If you are multiplying two or more Decomposed Variables together, you need have a lot less certainty in the resultant product that has been computed
#4	If there is uncertainty in just one Decomposed Variable, then the statistical-based ratio of the Upper Bound and Lower Bound values must be less than that of the original Decomposed Variable
#5	Avoid any sort of overlap between the Decomposed Variables. This greatly diminishes the value that has been set forth by the Decomposition Process at hand
#6	If you can create a statistical-based distribution with the data you have at hand (whether it is quantitative or qualitative in nature, or even a combination of both), there is really no need to conduct an exhaustive Decomposition process, as this only further diminish the value of it

A Critical Variable Related to Cyber Risk: Reputational Damage

After a company has been impacted by a major Cybersecurity attack, one of the issues that needs to be addressed quickly, and is often done at the last of BC, is that of trying to control the amount of reputational loss that has occurred. This is more of a nebulous term to define, but some examples of this include the following:

- Loss of customers;
- Damage to brand;
- Share price of the company deteriorating because of sharp sell offs by shareholders;
- Lost sales and revenues;
- Tarnished public image;
- Loss of loyalty by existing customers switching over to the competition;
- Negative media coverage;
- Civil and/or criminal-based lawsuits;
- Audits and/or compliance fees leveraged by the CCPA, GDPR, HIPPA, etc.;
- Etc.

It should be noted that Reputational Damage is more of a long-term impact rather than a short-term one. Therefore, the error in thinking here is that this is an item that can be done at the last of the BC plan. However, Reputational Damage starts at the moment of the impact of the Cybersecurity attack and needs to be addressed quickly, before the losses even exceed the direct costs created by the Cyberattack in the first place.

In order to deal with this, the CISO and his/her IT Security team need to engage in what are known as "Penance Projects". This is where certain allocations of funding are made to each of the major Reputational Damages just described. In other words, there is a separate bucket of money that has been set aside to try to contain the damage that has been caused due to Reputational Damages after a Cyberattack has occurred.

Thus, these efforts tend to be much more subjective in nature and some examples include the following:

- Public relation campaign pushes and efforts in an effort to convince both internal and external stakeholders that serious

efforts are being taken on a real-time basis in order to mitigate any further risk or damage that can occur because of the
Cyberattack;
- Marketing and advertising campaigns to convince existing
customers and any new prospects to stay on board with their
dedication to continue to purchase from the company that has
been impacted by the Cyberattack because of current efforts
that are underway to determine the underlying cause of what
has happened and the necessary controls that will be put into
place in order to correct this problem.

How to Reduce the Level of Cyber Risk with Bayesian Techniques

So far in this chapter, we have presented various concepts, terms,
methods, Excel-based formulas, and matrices in order to help you to
determine your particular level of Cyber Risk. Most important is that
the whole purpose of calculating your organization's particular level of
Cyber Risk is to help you formulate a certain strategy to lessen or even
mitigate that Cyber Risk just calculated. Remember that in the world
of Cybersecurity, the primary objective is to always keep your level of
Cyber Risk as low as possible to whatever is applicable in your industry.

It is important to remember that each market vertical or industry
will have their own benchmark defining the permissible range of a
Cybersecurity Risk. It is thus very important that you stay within
these guidelines or ranges and to even stay as far away as you can
from the boundaries. This not only translates to the fact that particular lines of defenses will be beefed up, but also that if you can
prove to your C-Suite and Board of Directors that you indeed have a
lower level of Cybersecurity Risk when compared to your peers, you
will probably have a greater chance of being heard by them and getting more funding for your Cyber Budgets, which in today's time are
very tight in view of the COVID-19 pandemic. Remember that your
level of Cyber Risk can be calculated by making use of quantitative or
qualitative variables and methods. But as far as possible, it is always
best to try to make use of the quantitative approaches, as this leaves
the least Margin of Error in case you are ever questioned about them.

Thus so far in this chapter, we have also introduced a quantitative
approach with what is known as the "Bayesian Methods". This

methodology has a number of distinct advantages which include the following:

- It is a very well-established methodology, having its roots in Statistical-based concepts and theories for a very long time;
- It makes usage of both the knowledge and findings of key experts in this particular field;
- Given the power of the Bayesian methods, you do not need a whole lot of data in which to make some well-justified findings about your current level of Cybersecurity Risk;
- The various Statistical methods that reside from within the Bayesian Framework are actually quite resilient in nature – even the most minute tweaks and changes in the "What If Scenarios" as played out by the CISO and their IT Security team can be reflected very quickly, even in Excel-based spreadsheets.

In the next subsection, we examine some of the most critical Statistical concepts and principles that your company can make use of when it comes to calculating your level of Cybersecurity and bringing it down to an acceptable form to the CISO, and most importantly, the Board of Directors.

The Important Statistical Concepts of the Bayesian Theory

Here are some of the most important ones that you will need to know as your organization tries to determine its overall leverage of Cybersecurity Risk:

1) The Probability

In this regard, $P(A)$ is the Statistical Probability that event "A" will actually happen. It is important to note that this value has to be somewhere from 0 to 1, and it must also be mutually inclusive. The Statistical Inverse of this is denoted as $P(-A)$. For instance, if a major Security Breach were to occur, this would be represented as $P(SB)$, and the chances of it not happening would be $P(-SB)$, where SB = Security Breach.

2) Two or more events can be true, but if one is contradictory, then one event cannot be true

In this kind of Cyber-related scenario, all of the Statistical Probabilities of both Mutually Exclusive and Inclusive Cyber-related events must add up the Absolute Value of "1". In the case of just two events, this can be mathematically represented as follows:

$$P(A) + P(-A) = 1$$

In other words, only one particular event can happen and not the other, especially if they both contradict one another.

3) The Statistical Probability of more than one event occurring

In this instance, P(A,B), both Cyber events (denoted as "A" and "B", respectively) are true, and thus, the likelihood that they will happen are very real. But this is assuming that Cyber-related events are both mutually Inclusive of each other. If in the chance that they are independent from one another - meaning one event is not dependent on the other and there is no further relationship in the Decomposition Process as reviewed earlier in this chapter, then this can be mathematically represented as follows:

$$P(A)P(B)$$

4) The Statistical Probability when two or more events are dependent upon each other

This dependent functionality can be mathematically represented as follows:

$$P(A|B)$$

In this certain instance, both Cyber-related events (denoted as "A" and "B", respectively) are both Mathematically and Statistically dependent upon one another. In other words, if one event were to occur, then the other must happen first or in tandem with the another, as the variables that are contained in both of them are catalysts for each of the other event to happen first.

5) How to break up simultaneous events into a series of events

In this particular instance, the assumption is that there is more than one Cyber event that is happening in real time and that they all are occurring at more or less the same time frames of one another. But, what if you want to break up these Cyber-related ones into independent ones, so that they can be examined and further analyzed in much more detail? Well, this can be done using principles of the Bayesian Methodology and can mathematically represented as:

$$P\left(A, B, C\right) = P\left(A\,|\,,B\,|\,,C\right) * P\left(B, C\right) * P\left(C\right)$$

In terms of Statistical-based nomenclature, this is also known as the "Chain Rule". In this scenario, A, B, and C are all Cyber-related events that are occurring among one another at about the same time.

6) <u>How to add up different events that are not related to another</u>
In the world of Cybersecurity, there is a great likelihood that two events that are totally unrelated to each other could still have some type or kind of bearing which in the end can influence the outcome of what is to happen in the end. For example, the results of a Penetration Test could have some bearing if a security breach were to occur, especially if the remediative actions that were proposed by the Penetration Testing team were not followed through by the CISO and the IT Security team. This can be mathematically represented as:

$$P(A) = P\left(A\,|\,B\right) * P\left(B\right) + P\left(A\,|\sim B\right) * P\left(\sim B\right)$$

7) <u>How to flip two simultaneous events</u>
As has been previously discussed, it is quite possible that two more Cyber-related events could be happening more or less in the same time frame of each other, but they can be further separated out from one another for further analyses. But what if the CISO and their IT Security team want to put some logic into how these events can be separated from one another, meaning that there is some casual relationship that exists between them, and they do not occur just together just by chance? This can be mathematically represented as:

$$P\left(A\,|\,B\right) = /\left(\mathrm{PB}\right)$$

where A and B are two Cyber-related events. In this case, P(A | B) can also be written as P(B | A).

But, here is where the trick lies. The above mathematical formula also allows for the Decomposition Process to take place, which takes into account two Decomposed variables for one Cyber-related event. If this were to be the case, then this is mathematically represented as:

$$P\Big(A\,|\,B\Big) = P\Big(A\Big) * P\Big(B\,|\,A\Big)$$
$$/ \Big[P\Big(B\,|\,A\Big) * P\Big(A\Big) + P\Big(B\,|\sim A\Big) * P\Big(\sim A\Big) \Big]$$

Making Use of Prior Cyber Events in the Bayesian Methodology

It must be noted here that before the Bayes Methodologies can be applied, there must be some kind of inputs that are available to feed into the statistical models that arise from it. As we have mentioned before, this is literally "Garbage In and Garbage Out". But you may be asking at this point where will you get these inputs from? Well, they are going to come from both the qualitative and quantitative factors that you have computed, and most likely, this will be done by the CISO and his/her IT Security team. In statistical terms, this can be defined more technically as "Informative based Prior Events".

The reason for the term "Prior" being attached is that the inputs are used to predict the Cybersecurity Threat Landscape or to assess a certain condition have been previously computed, whether they are simply numbers or even including expert opinion. There is also another term called an "Uninformative Prior". This is the case where the CISO and their IT Security team can only make an estimate (especially only if qualitative inputs can be used). Any further refinements can be made to it as more quantitative data is being used to further refine it. In this case, the "Uninformed Prior" will have the maximum or an extremely high threshold of uncertainty.

On the flip side, there is then the term "Informative Prior", and as its name implies, this is just the complete opposite of the

"Uninformative Prior". In this situation, the values of all the quantitative inputs are known with a very high level of certainty, and those of the qualitative ones as well. This can also be deemed to be a higher risk approach because the CISO and his/her IT Security team is taking a huge "Leap of Faith" when it comes to the inputs that they have calculated.

Put in another way, there are no other permutation they are taking into consideration. These can also be referred to as "Calibrated Estimates". But with the "Uniformed Priors", many more permutations are taken into consideration and is a much more conservative, cautious approach than is usually taken. In a contradictory sense of the term, the CISO and his/her IT Security team are taking a higher level of risk with the "Informative Prior" approach to bring down the overall level of Cyber Risk that their company is exposed to at that current point in time.

Statistically Proving the Bayesian Theorem

In a previous subsection in this chapter, we introduced a concept known as the "Chain Rule". This very same concept can actually be used to statistically prove the Bayesian Theorem (it has also been referred to in this chapter in "Methodology").

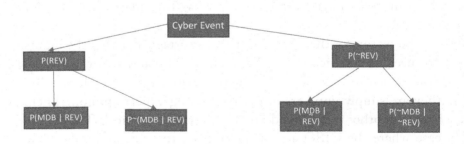

The statistical formulas are as follows:

- P(MDB, REV) = P(REV, MDB): This is also known as the "Commutative Property";
- P(MDB, REV) = P(MDB) * P(REV | MDB). This represents the First Branch;

- P(REV, MDB) = P(REV) * P(MDB | REV). This represents Branches 1 and 2;
- P(MDB) * P(REV | MDB) = P(REV) * P(MDB | REV). This represents Branches 1, 2, and 3.

The Applications of the Bayesian Methodology

In this subsection, we look at some examples of using the Bayesian Methodology in some real-word Cyber Events. But first, it is important to illustrate the probabilities that will be used, and these are exemplified in Tables 1.5 and 1.6.

Here are some key points to be made about these two tables:

- Table 1.5 represents the Calibrated Estimates;
- Table 1.6 represents the Derived Values (Also referred to earlier in a previous subsection as the "Uniformed Priors".)

Table 1.7 describes the variables that have been used.

Table 1.5   Probabilities Used In The Bayesian Statistical Modeling

THE CYBER EVENT	THE PROBABILITY
P(MDB | REV)	25.00%
P(MDB | ~REV)	1.00%
P(REV | PPT)	95.00%
P(REV | ~PPT)	0.05%
P(PPT)	1.00%

Table 1.6   Probabilities Used In The Bayesian Statistical Modeling

THE CYBER EVENT	THE PROBABILITY
P(REV | MDB)	25.15%
P(REV | ~MDB)	0.76%
P(~MDB | REV)	75.00%
P(MDB)	1.24%
P(REV)	1.00%
P(MDB | PPT)	23.80%
P(MDB | ~PPT)	1.01%

Table 1.7 The Cyber Variables Used In Bayesian Statistical Modeling

THE VARIABLE	WHAT IT STANDS FOR
MDB	Massive Data Breach
REV	Remotely Exploitable Vulnerability
PPT	Positive Penetration Test
P	Probability of Cyber Event

These numbers and definitions can now be used to illustrate how the Bayesian Methodology can be used to calculate the Statistical Probability of some Cyber-related event actually happening:

1) The Statistical Probability of an REV in occurring
   This can be mathematically represented as follows:

$$P(\text{REV}) = P(\text{PPT}) * \text{PREVs} | \text{PPT}) + P(\sim \text{PPT})$$
$$* P(\text{REV}) \;|\sim \text{PPT})$$
$$(.01) * (0.95) + \left(1 - .01\right) * (.0005) = 1.0\%$$

2) The Statistical Probability of an MDB in occurring
   This can be mathematically represented as follows:

$$P(\text{MDB}) = P(\text{REV}) * P\left(\text{MDB} | \text{REV}\right) + P(\sim \text{REV})$$
$$* P\left(\text{MDB} |\sim \text{REV}\right)$$
$$(.01) * (0.25) + \left(1 - .01\right) * (.01) = 1.24\%$$

3) The Statistical Probability of an REV as a Result of a Massive MDB in Occurring
   This can be mathematically represented as follows:

$$P\left(\text{REV} | \text{MDB}\right) = P\left(\text{MDB} | \text{REV}\right) * P(\text{REV}) / P(\text{MDB})$$
$$(.25) * (0.01) / (.0124) = 20.16\%$$

4) The Statistical Probability of an REV as a Result of a Massive MDB in **NOT** Occurring
   This can be mathematically represented as follows:

$$P\left(\text{REV} |\sim \text{MDB}\right) = P\left(\sim \text{MDB} | \text{REV}\right) * P(\text{REV}) / P(\sim \text{MDB})$$
$$(1 - 0.25) * (0.01) / + \left(1 - 0.0124\right) = 0.76\%$$

5) <u>The Statistical Probability of an MDB as a Result of a Positive</u>
<u>PPT</u>

This can be mathematically represented as follows:

$$P\left(\text{MDB}\,|\,\text{PPT}\right) = P\left(\text{REV}\,|\,\text{PPT}\right) * P\left(\text{MDB}\,|\,\text{REV}\right)$$
$$+ \left(1 - P\left(\text{REV}\,|\,\text{PPT}\right)\right) * P\left(\text{MDB}\,|\,\sim\text{REV}\right)$$
$$\left(0.95\right) * \left(0.25\right) + \left(.05\right) * \left(.01\right) = 23.8\%$$

6) <u>The Statistical Probability of an MDB as Result of a **Negative**</u>
<u>PPT</u>

This can be mathematically represented as follows:

$$P\left(\text{MDB}\,|\,\sim\text{PPT}\right) = P\left(\text{REV}\,|\,\sim\text{PPT}\right) * P\left(\text{MDB}\,|\,\text{REV}\right)$$
$$+ \left(1 - P\left(\text{REV}\,|\,\sim\text{PPT}\right)\right) * P\left(\text{MDB}\,|\,\sim\text{REV}\right)$$
$$\left(0.0005\right) * \left(0.25\right) + \left(.05\right) * \left(1 - .0005\right) * \left(.01\right) = 1.01\%$$

It is interesting to note that those events that are dual in nature and that in which both have an impact on a company seem to have a much higher probability in happening than just the single events, or those dual events in which one does not cause the other to occur. These are illustrated in Cases #3 and #5.

How to Reduce the Level of Cyber Risk with More Sophisticated Bayesian Techniques

In the world of Cybersecurity, the gathering of information and data is always a daily must. For example, it is these datasets that are fed into the AI and ML tools in order to get a realistic grasp as to what the Cybersecurity Threat Landscape could look like in the future. Also, most if not all IT Security teams today in Corporate America are totally inundated with filtering for false positives; having robust information/datasets will be a huge boon in this regard as well.

But it is also very important to keep in mind that all of the needed information and data may not always be available, especially when it is needed the most. But fortunately, predictions and even mitigating the level of Cyber Risk that a particular company is exposed to can be extrapolated from merely a few Data

Points. This can be achieved using a Statistical-based concept that is known as the "Beta Distribution". This is yet another very powerful component of the Bayesian Methodology. This and other very important Statistical-based Theorems will be presented in this subsection.

The Beta Distribution

In the world of Statistics, the Beta Distribution is very used to explain sizes in the human population. This is technically referred to as the "Population Proportion". In other words, this is just a certain segment of the entire population that falls into some specific type of Statistical-based subset. But what is very powerful about the concept of the Beta Distribution is that only a very small sample size can be used to get a snapshot of the entire population as a whole. Put in much simpler terms, it only takes a little to discover or prove a lot. So how can this all be further applied to the world of Cybersecurity? Suppose that a company wants to compare its particular of Cyber Risk to that of its industry peers. But for some reason or another, not a lot of organizations in this certain industry are actually forthcoming about their own, particular level of Cyber Risk. Well, this is where the Beta Distribution can come into play. Even if the CISO and their IT Security team can just get a handful of samples, they will still be able to get a rather solid, scientific aspect as to where they stand in the rest of the crowd when it comes to the level of Cyber Risk.

So how can this be done? Well, in the Beta Distribution, there are two components to it. The first is called the "Alpha". In and Excel, the mathematical formula for this is as follows:

$$= \text{Betadist}\left(p, \text{Alpha}, \text{Beta}\right)$$

where

X = That proportion of the population (or sample size) that needs to be tested.

The Statistical-based Inverse for the Beta Distribution is defined technically as the "Inverse Probability Function", and to compute this in Excel, the mathematical formula is thus defined as:

$$= \text{Betainv}\left(x, \text{Alpha}, \text{Beta}\right)$$

where

P = The proportion of the population (or sample size) that is deemed to be just high enough so that there is a certain Probabilistic Level that this sample of the population that is being studied is actually lower.

But the key trick here that you have to keep in mind is that in order to compute both the Alpha and Beta, you need to have just one Probability Distribution that has been computed previously. Since this is a quantitative Measure, this can also be referred to as an "Informed Prior", as discussed earlier in this chapter. Qualitative variables and estimates can also be used as well, but more of them will be needed if you want to achieve a Uniform Statistical Distribution of anywhere in the range from 0% to 100%.

But if the latter approach is utilized, then both the Alpha and Beta values in the above-mentioned formulas must be set to a Numerical Value of "1". This simply translates to the fact that there is hardly any previous information and/or data that is available to the CISO and their IT Security team at that particular point in time. All of this can also be graphically displayed with what is known as a "Probability Density Function". In this regard, the area under the bell shaped curve that is produced actually represents or sums up to a Numerical Value of "1". Mathematically, this is represented as:

$$= \text{Betadist}\left(x, \text{prior alpha}, + \text{hits}, \text{prior beta} + \text{misses}\right)$$

But in the real world of Cybersecurity, we always want to get as many Data Points as possible, even if it means just getting a very small subset. So, if we get more than one, the mathematical formula for representing this uptick is:

$$= \text{Beta}\left(x + i / 2, \text{prior alpha} + \text{hits}, \text{prior beta} + \text{misses}\right)$$
$$- \text{betadist}\left(x - i / 2, \text{prior alpha} + \text{hits}, \text{prior beta} + \text{misses}\right)$$

In this regard, even if you want to know something like "Out of 6 security breaches that could occur to Company XYZ, what are the chances that it will be a Ransomware based attack?" This is where yet another Statistical Concept called the "Binomial Distribution" comes into play. This is very similar to the Beta Distribution, but the primary difference here is that with this, you are using prior Inputs. But with the Binomial Distribution, you are using actually estimating either the quantitative or the qualitative values of the Inputs that you are planning to make use of. If you are going to use Excel to calculate the Binomial Distribution, the mathematical formula for doing so is represented as:

$$= \text{binmdist}\left(\text{hits, sample size, probability, } 0\right)$$

where

The Numerical Value of "0": This represents the Statistical Probability of an exact outcome, not just an estimated one.

Making Use of the Log Odds Ratio

There is yet another method that is available for predicting the level of Cyber Risk that your company is currently at, and from there, how the CISO and their IT Security team can leverage ways in which to bring lower that particular level as possible. This is technically known as the "Log Odds Ratio", also "LOR" for short. This method in some ways is much more sophisticated than some other Statistical-based methods we have examined so far in this chapter. The primary reason for this is that with the Log Odds Ratio, each input that you are using first to calculate your level of Cyber Risk can be examined first separately and then summated altogether at the end.

This actually is a variant of another sophisticated Statistical-based method that is known as "Logistic Regression". This technique is primarily used when you have large amounts of datasets to filter through, such as those that are related to Big Data and Data Warehousing. So in the real world of Cybersecurity, this would obviously be a much better tool to use, given the fact information and data are collected on a 24 X 7 X 365 basis. In its simplest form, the Log Odds ration can be mathematically represented as follows:

$$P(x) = \log\left[P(x)/1 - (P(x))\right]$$

where

P(x) = The overall probability of your Cyber Risk falling within a certain range.

However, there are some caveats to keep in mind here:

- This technique will not give you a specific number for your level of Cyber Risk; rather it will give you a range in which it could possible fall within. This is dependent upon the total number of inputs that you use. The more you have the better as this will give you a much tighter range to fall in versus using just one input, which will give you a very large range.
- This particular technique can be used for either quantitative inputs or qualitative inputs.

In the end, no matter what kind of inputs that the CISO and their IT Security team make use of, the following is a generalized approach as to how you should make use of the Log Odds Ratio Methodology, which is reviewed in detail in the next subsection.

How to Use the Log Odds Ratio (LOR) Methodology

1) When you conduct your specific Risk Analysis, use some sort of Categorization Scale that lets you determine the vulnerability of each Digital Asset in terms of being impacted by a security breach. This will be denoted as P(Event).

2) Once you have determined the above-mentioned Vulnerability Level, then try to assign a Statistical Probability to each Digital Asset that it will or won't be impacted by a Cyberattack. The key differences between the Vulnerability Level and the Statistical Probability is that with the former, you are showing the level of weakness that it currently possesses, even with all of the controls in place. It is important to note that all Digital Assets will have some degree of weakness; some of them will have it more than the others. The latter demonstrates how prone an asset is to a Cyberattack. Thus, a weaker Digital

Asset will be more prone to a Cyberattack versus one that has stronger controls that are associated with it. In the end here, the Statistical Probability will be denoted as P(E | X).

3) Now, convert the Statistical Probabilities that have computed in the last step (which are known technically now as the "Baseline Probabilities") into the "Conditional Probabilities" that can be used for a Log Odds Ratio model. This can be mathematically represented as:

$$\text{LOR}\left[P(\text{Event})\right] = \ln\left[P(\text{Event})\right] / \left[1 - P(\text{Event})\right]$$

$$= \ln\left(.02 / .98 = -3.89182\right); \text{LOR}\left[P\left(\text{Event} \mid \text{Sensitive Data}\right)\right]$$

$$= \ln\left(.04 / 0.06\right) = -3.17805$$

This iterative cycle must continue for each level of input that you are using, regardless of it being quantitative or qualitative. Also keep in mind that the above numbers are for illustrative purposes only.

4) Next, you now need to compute what is technically known as the "Delta LOR" for each input that you are using for the LOR Model. Put in simpler terms, this is merely the Mathematical Subtraction of the Conditional-based LOR from the Baseline-established LOR, as this was determined in Steps #2 and #3.

5) Continue with Step #4 for each input that you have, whether it is quantitative or qualitative.

6) Now, compute both the "Adjusted LOR" and the "Adjusted Probability". This is done with the following mathematical formulas:

$$\text{The Adjusted LOR} : -3.89 + 0.71 + 0.19 - 0.45 + 1.02 = -2.42$$

$$\text{The Adjusted Probability} : 1 / \left[1 + 1 / \exp\left(-2.42\right)\right] = 0.08167$$

Note: The above numbers are for illustrative purposes only.

The Lens Methodology

Apart from the other Statistical-based Methodologies we have reviewed so far in this chapter, there is yet another technique that is devoted to gathering information with the sole purpose of just computing the Statistical Values that are associated strictly with the qualitative inputs when they are used by the CISO and their IT Security team when it comes to figuring the organization's particular level of Cyber Risk. This is known specifically as the "Lens Methodology".

The subsequent list is an outline of the steps that you need to take in order to make good use of it:

1) Identify the people in your company who are well versed in the knowledge of past security breaches if they have occurred in your company. This will typically include mostly members of the IT Security team and others from other departments that may have been impacted as well.

2) Ask each and every individual about the relevant factors associated with the impacted items – this will of course be mostly the Digital Assets.

3) From these factors, try to come up with a list of all possible threat variants that could impact these same Digital Assets again. It is important to note that you will be also making use of predicted future events to do this (such as the outcomes that have been predicted by AI- and ML-based tools).

4) Ask these people you have identified as to what the Statistical Probabilities are for these same Digital Assets if hit again but with newer threat variants.

5) Take the average of these Statistical Probabilities.

6) In this last step, you will be making use of another Statistical Methodology which is known as "Logistic Regression Analysis". In this case, you will formulate one Dependent Variable (known as "Y") and various other Independent Variables (known as "X"). The former will just be the final average of all of the Statistical Probabilities and the latter will be the possible range of threat variants that could impact that one Digital Asset that was breached before.

7) Once you have completed the modelling process, a resultant graph will then be computed and displayed (assuming that you are using Excel for this approach). Once the best plot has been computed for all of the relevant Data Points, this will then become technically known as the "Lens Model".

A Cross Comparison of the LOR and Lens Methodologies

Table 1.8 describes the differences between the two.

As one can see from Table 1.8, if the CISO and their IT Security team need to get a feel of where the level of Cyber Risk is at a current point in time, then the LOR Methodology will work best. However, if time is not an issue and a much more comprehensive and holistic approach is needed, then the Lens Method will be the best choice to make use of in this circumstance. There are also some other obstacles to using both of these methods, and they are given subsequently:

- The issue of "Correlation Neglect": This happens when the dependent variables in the Logistic Regression Model display a high level of Statistical-based Correlation. This could lead to a very serious impediment in making judgments for the future, especially when it comes to the specific formulation and deployment of the needed controls. This issue of high Correlation is known technically as "Multicollinearity".
- Initially, there can be a sharp misunderstanding of how these two Methodologies work; thus one prefers not using them at all.
- With the Lens Method, a strong intent of merely establishing Statistical Probabilities could very well exist, thus impeding any other judgments or observations that need to be made.
- A desire for more information and data to be provided could also exist, thus giving more than what is needed. The end resultant is that any other subsequent inputs could thus be highly skewed and/or biased.

Table 1.8 A Cross Comparison of Bayesian Statistical Methodologies

THE LOR METHODOLOGY	THE LENS METHOD
Takes a lesser time to complete	This takes more time as this requires inputs from various individuals
This is simpler to use	More complex because a Regression Model is needed
Gives outputs with *more variation* in the Statistical Estimates	Gives outputs with *less variation* in the Statistical Estimates
Reduces inconsistency	Reduces inconsistency, but provides other avenues for gauging the actual level

How to Ascertain the Value of Information and Data

Another common theme that has been detailed quite a bit in this chapter is that there is a lot of information and data available in the world of Cybersecurity. To make it even more complex, this kind and/or type of information/data will more than likely greatly vary upon which realm of Cybersecurity you are dealing with. It is important to keep in mind that it is a big world out there. But the bottom line is that not all of this information and data really have much value. So, the next big question is about trying to determine your particular of Cyber Risk and what kind of value you put against it?

Here are some mathematical formulas that the CISO and their IT Security team can use when trying to compute this. First, there is what is known as the "Expected Opportunity Loss", or also known as the "EOL" for short. This can be represented as:

The Financial Cost of Being Wrong
*The Statistical Probability of Being Wrong

In its simplest terms, the true value of information and data is just the sheer reduction of the Expected Opportunity Loss. But in the theoretical sense, if the EOL is completely "O" (this is the situation where all levels of Cyber Risk are completely eradicated). This is technically known as the "Expected Value of Perfect Information" or "EVPI" for short. Now we know that in the real world of Cybersecurity that this can never happen, so the EVPI is a much more useful measure for gauging what the Statistical Upper Limit could potentially be if some newer pieces of information and data were brought to the table. In the end, any value that is associated with information and data will be primarily contingent upon the key decisions that are being made by the CISO and their IT Security team to assign a level to their particular Cyber Risk.

So for example, if you choose to implement a Next Generation Firewall/VPN to further beef up your lines of defenses, the "Financial Cost of Being Wrong" is merely the money that has been spent upon procuring and deploying it, when it really was not needed. Now on the flip side, if you did not implement this and your organization suffered a security breach, then this will become your "Statistical Probability of Being Wrong".

How a Known Factor Can Have an Impact on a Predicted Event

In the world of Cybersecurity, trying to predict what the Threat Landscape will look like in the future with newer variants coming out is probably one of the areas of great interest to the CISO and their IT Security team. Trying to do this all by hand would obviously be a nightmare, and not only that, it would take an enormous time to compute. So by the time the computations are done, it is quite likely that the potential threat variants have now become real ones. But also as mentioned previously in this chapter, this is where the specific roles of both AI and ML tools will come into play.

But just to give you an idea as to how all of this can be done, suppose you have collected some sample data that consists primarily of a security event that has affected a Database Server. Then, based upon that, you have made some further extrapolations as to what could potentially happen on that same Database Server. To keep things simple, only one event is being used, so the values are either "0" (which means nothing has happened or will happen) and/or "1" (which means something has happened or will happen again into the future).

Table 1.9 depicts this.

So, if the CISO and their IT Security team want to compute the Conditional Probability of an event happening based upon a prior one that has occurred, the mathematical formula for doing this in Excel is:

$$= \text{countifs}\left(\text{column } A, "=1", \text{column } B, "=1\right) / \text{countif}\left(\text{column } B, "=?1"\right)$$

Table 1.9 The Statistical Events of a Cyber Impact to a Database

THE DEFINED SECURITY THAT OCCURRED ON THE DATABASE SERVER (COLUMN A)	THE STATED CONDITION THAT OCCURRED ON THE DATABASE SERVER (COLUMN B)
1	0
1	1
0	0
0	1
1	1
1	1
0	1

A Brief Overview of Cybersecurity Metrics

In just about every profession that one can imagine, there is one common denominator: Metrics and Key Performance Indicators (KPIs). Although there weren't too many of these in existence in the past in Cybersecurity, it is now taking the center stage, given the COVID-19 pandemic. Not only CISOs and their IT Security teams are being judged by this, but also ever tightening budgets are also based upon them. A good example of this is the level of Cyber Risk that your company is currently experiencing. If you can prove to the C-Suite and to your Board of Directors that this particular threat is actually emerging, then there is a reasonably good chance that you can get your budget increased. In the end, it just all comes down to making sure that the constrained financial resources are being used in the most strategic ways possible.

But of course, it is impossible to use all of the Metrics and KPIs that are out there for the CISO and the IT Security team. Therefore, careful thought and consideration have to be given as to the right ones which need to be used. It is also important to keep in mind that many of these Metrics and KPIs are found in what are known as "Cybersecurity Frameworks". Probably some of the best known ones are that which have been created by the National Institute of Standards and Technology (NIST). A "Cybersecurity Framework" can be defined as follows:

> A cybersecurity framework is a series of documents defining the best practices an organization follows to manage its cybersecurity risk. Such frameworks reduce a company's exposure to vulnerabilities.[6]

In other words, it is more like a template that guides the CISO and their IT Security team into ascertaining not only which of those KPIs and Metrics will work best for them, but also give them the ability to conduct a Risk Assessment Analysis, and from there, formulate a list of controls that can be used to further bring down their particular level of Cyber Risk. From this Cybersecurity Framework, they will also be in a much better position to adopt a distinct list of Standards and Best Practices as well. Although it is out of the scope of this chapter to examine all of these, we will just examine a few of them in closer detail, especially in the way how they relate to Cyber Risk.

Here is a brief survey into them:

1) The Operational Security Metrics Maturity Model

    This is also known as the "OSMMM". In general terms, this Model (also keep in mind that Frameworks can also be referred to as "Cybersecurity Frameworks") primarily consists of a list of standardized templates and questions in an effort to guide the CISO and their IT Security team in the activities just previously described.

2) The Sparse Data Analytics Model

    This is also referred to as the "SDAM". There is a specific usage for this kind of Cybersecurity Framework when the ability for the CISO and their IT Security team to collect a wide range of information and data is low and scarce, both from a qualitative and quantitative perspective. This kind of methodology is employed when a company is making a first attempt at calculating their particular level of Cyber Risk, and from there, deciding how their Cybersecurity Budget should be spent in bringing that level of risk down.

3) The Functional Security Metrics Model

    This is also known as the "FSMM". This kind of Cybersecurity Framework is used when the CISO and their IT Security team have determined their level of Cyber Risk, and are now ready to test come controls to see hypothetically how that level of Cyber Risk can be further reduced. Overall, there are two major branches of KPIs and Metrics that fit into this Cybersecurity Framework, which are as follows:

    • Coverage and Configuration Metrics

        These are the KPIs which are used to test and confirm the Operational Effectiveness of the controls that you are considering of implementing in the Production Environment at your business. Drilling down further, they deal with how more with the Configuration aspects of the controls, in an effort to make sure that they are optimized in the best possible way.

- Mitigation Metrics

  These are the KPIs that measure just how well the newly deployed controls are functioning in terms of mitigating that particular level of Cyber Risk not only just at the present time, but in the future as well.

4) The Security Data Marts Model

This is also known as the "SDMM". This specific Cybersecurity Framework is used in a much more cross-functional approach when compared to the other three Frameworks just reviewed. For example, the Metrics and the KPIs that are formulated here are used across the People, Processes, and Technology processes across an entire organization. Specific examples of this Framework used are as follows:

- How long a threat variant (or for that matter even a Cyberattacker) is lingering in your IT and Network Infrastructure until it is formally detected;
- The calculation of what is known as "Residual Cybersecurity Risk". This is the amount of Cyber Risk that is still remaining after the initial level of it has been curtailed with the newly deployed controls.

5) The Prescriptive Analytics Model

This is also known as the "PAM". This is actually a newly created Cybersecurity Framework, and it consists of three distinct realms which are as follows:

- Descriptive Analytics

  This area deals more with those KPIs and Metrics that are much descriptive in nature, as opposed to those that are much more quantitative.

- Predictive Analytics

  This aspect involves predicting what the future Cybersecurity Threat Landscape will look like making use of already established quantitative and qualitative inputs. A key concept here is that of what is known as "Statistical Prioritization". This is where the CISO and their IT Security team need to decide which of these inputs to use in an effective and efficient fashion, rather than just simply dumping all of the inputs into an AI or ML system.

- Prescriptive Analytics
  This takes into account both the above two mentioned areas from which a single, cohesive platform can be created and launched in which multiple models, both quantitative and qualitative ones, can be run simultaneously, in an effort to gauge what the Cybersecurity Threat Landscape will look like in the future.

Our next chapter will examine the specific Controls that the CISO and their IT Security team can adopt into their own business environment in an effort to further mitigate their particular of Cyber Risk.

Notes

1 "How to Measure Anything In Cybersecurity Risk". Daniel Geer and Stuart McClure. John Wiley and Sons, 2016.
2 https://stats.idre.ucla.edu/other/mult-pkg/faq/general/faq-what-is-the-coefficient-of-variation/
3 https://mixpanel.com/topics/statistical-significance/
4 https://www.investopedia.com/terms/s/standarddeviation.asp
5 https://www.statisticshowto.com/lognormal-distribution/
6 https://reciprocitylabs.com/resources/what-is-a-cybersecurity-framework/

2

CYBERSECURITY AUDITS, FRAMEWORKS, AND CONTROLS

Chapter 1 reviewed in rather extensive detail what Cybersecurity Risk is all about and some of the relevant Statistical-based models and techniques that the CISO and their IT Security team can use rather efficiently and quickly on a real-time basis. It is important that in order to deploy the concepts and methodologies discussed in Chapter 1, an organization does not necessarily have to have an Artificial Intelligence (AI) or Machine Learning (ML) environment in place.

Rather, these concepts and methodologies can be quickly deployed making use of Microsoft Excel. The only real disadvantage of this is that it can be a rather time-consuming process to get the desired outputs that are needed.

Unfortunately, this time lag can mean the difference between being hit by a security breach or not. Therefore, over time and as the need for them further proliferates, the CISO and his/her IT Security team should take very seriously the procurement and deployment of both AI and ML tools in order to compensate for this time lag, as the processing of the information and data can happen on a real-time basis.

Another key advantage of making use of both of these tools is that they can both filter out the false positives that are being outputted.

The end result of this is that the IT Security team will be alleviated of the pressure to filter through all of this, thus giving them the critical time that is needed to use only those legitimate pieces of information and data that will be prove to be extremely useful in calculating that particular Cybersecurity Risk for their organization.

But, it should also be noted very strongly here that making use of both AI and ML tools are only as good as the information and data that are fed into them in order to calculate this level of Cybersecurity Risk.

DOI: 10.1201/9781003023685-2

For example, if the information and data are not optimized and cleaned on a daily basis according to the stringent requirements set forth by the CISO and their IT Security team, the outputs will then be highly skewed, thus giving a false sense and indication of the particular level of Cybersecurity Risk that has been gauged and calculated. In other words, it is merely "Garbage In and Garbage Out". The tools are only as good as what is fed into them.

So therefore, the CISO and their IT Security team must give consideration to all of this and must make use of both extremely reliable and optimized datasets from very reputable Cyber Intelligence Feeds in order to make sure that you are gauging the most accurate level of Cyber Risk that is possible.

As also discussed to a great extent in the previous chapter, the information and data that are used to calculate Cyber Risk can be both quantitative and/or qualitative in nature. But the bottom line once again is that whatever is used, it must be that the information and data be trusted across all levels and that they can also be credible under the scrutiny of both the C-Suite and the Board of Directors.

An Overview of the Cybersecurity Controls

Now that the roots of what Cyber Risk actually are has been established, it is now time to turn our attention to something that is closely allied with Cybersecurity Risk. And that is, the Controls that are put into place. You may be asking at this point what exactly a Control is. Well, this question will not be only answered, but it will be examined in detail in this chapter, which is its main focus.

But to give you a broad idea of what it is, a Cybersecurity Control (also referred to in this chapter as "Cyber Control") is a tool or mechanism that is used to help mitigate or bring down the level of Cyber Risk that a particular business is exposed to at a current point in time. It is important to keep in mind at this point that Cyber Risk can never be truly 100% eradicated.

If this were to be the case, then theoretically speaking, there would be no threat variants that would exist. But, reality dictates that Cyber Risk will always exist and the key mantra that the CISO and their IT Security team need to keep in mind is that it can only be reduced to certain level that is acceptable to them.

It is also very important to note here that the level of Cyber Risk is not just the result of one item at a particular point in time, but rather, it is the culmination of several levels of Risk that are posed to all of the digital assets of a particular organization.

For example, a company will have both digital and physical assets at hand. Each and every one of them will be vulnerable to a certain extent of being hit by a large scale Cyberattack. But to what degree is this vulnerability? As is also alluded to in Chapter 1, this is where the Risk Assessment Analysis comes into play. With this kind of study at hand, the CISO and their IT Security team are literally taking into consideration all of the assets that their company has, and by making use of a categorization, are ranking their degree of vulnerability or weakness on some pre-established categorization scale.

For example, it can be a scale that ranges from 1 to 10. In this particular instance, 1 would indicate the "Least Vulnerable", and 10 would indicate something like "Extremely Vulnerable" or "Most Vulnerable". Anything that is ranked in the intermediary, such as that with a value of "5" would be considered as an asset, whether digital or physical in nature, to be at a "Medium Vulnerability" level.

It is also very important to note here that while these values can be used to help calculate the particular level of Cyber Risk at which a company is, there are a plethora of other inputs and variables, both quantitative and qualitative, which need to be taken into consideration as well. This was also covered in great detail in Chapter 1.

But in the end, this categorization scale that was just illustrated can be used to clearly demonstrate what is weak and vulnerable, and those that are not and are much stronger in nature. In the end, obviously both those digital and physical assets that are the most prone to a Cybersecurity attack will have the most number of Controls that are assigned to them in order to bring down their level of Cyber Risk that they are contributing to the organization as a whole.

Those that are least prone will have some sort of Cyber Controls that are assigned to them, though probably not as numerous. And those that are deemed to be intermediary in nature in terms of weak or vulnerable ranking will have Cyber Controls that are also associated with them, but not too many and not too few, either.

This notion of making use of a Risk Assessment Analysis for illustrative purposes is extremely simplistic in nature. For example, it is a highly subjective call for the CISO and their IT Security team to determine what is weak and vulnerable and what is not. In other words, they are just making use of qualitative based best estimates, which are based upon the past experiences and knowledge that they possess.

In order to get a true and scientific assessment of what the actual level of vulnerability and weakness that each and every digital and physical asset possesses, a methodology known as the "Cybersecurity Audit" must first be conducted.

Only then can the appropriate Cyber Controls be determined and deployed. This is the topic for this next section of this chapter. Then from there, we will explore the various Cybersecurity Control Frameworks that are available, and from there, do a deeper dive into the individual Cybersecurity Controls that are available today.

A Technical Review of the Cybersecurity Audit

So far in this chapter we have covered the concept of what a Cybersecurity Audit is. But what exactly is it? It can be technically as defined as follows:

> Cybersecurity audits act as a checklist that organizations can use to validate their security policies and procedures. Organizations that conduct an audit will be able to assess whether or not they have the proper security mechanisms in place while also making sure they are in compliance with relevant regulations. This helps businesses take a proactive approach when designing cybersecurity policies, resulting in more dynamic threat management. Cybersecurity audits are performed by third-party vendors in order to eliminate any conflicts of interest. They can also be administered by an in-house team as long as they act independently of their parent organization.[1]

So as one can see from the above definition, the Cyber Audit can be viewed on a general level as a checklist that can be followed by the CISO and their IT Security team in order to make sure that all avenues have been covered with both the physical- and digital-based assets, at least when it comes to their vulnerabilities and weaknesses being addressed.

As the definition shows, proper actions can then be taken to make sure that all appropriate mechanisms are thus put in place, including the Controls to remediate the weaknesses and vulnerabilities that have been discovered as a result of doing the Cyber Audit. It is important to note here that there is typically no predefined process that is set forth to actually carry out the Cyber Audit and the procedures and events that follow thereafter.

All of this is highly dependent upon the security requirements of the organization in question, and the kinds and types of both physical and digital assets that it possesses. There is then the last component of the above-stated definition, which deals with who will actually carry out the Cyber Audit. This will be addressed later on this chapter. In a more technical sense, Cyber Audits can also be referred to as "Information Security Audits", as this is a much more encompassing term as to what the exact activities being carried out by the CISO and their IT Security team in this regard.

But for the purposes of this chapter, the term of "Cyber Audit" will be used. These Audits are held and conducted at time intervals that are planned well in advance, due to their intensity and the amount of attention that are involved. It can also be a very time-consuming process, depending upon how large the organization is, and the total number of both physical and digital assets. Now, the issue often arises as to who will conduct these Cyber Audits. They can be done in two distinct ways:

1) <u>Internally</u>

    While there may be others that are involved, it is typically the CISO and his or her IT Security team that will primarily conduct the Cyber Audit and be held responsible for the results that arises from it, and any action items to subsequently follow after that.

2) <u>Externally</u>

    This is where the company that wishes to do the Cyber Audit typically will hire an external third party for it. While there will be some significant financial cost to this, the primary advantage of doing it this way is that this external, third party will be impartial, objective, and unbiased upon what they discover in the Cyber Audit, as well as the recommendations that will subsequently come thereafter in order to remediate any weaknesses and vulnerabilities that are found in the physical- and digital-based assets. It should also be noted at this point that in this regard, a Cyber Audit team can consist of the Internal Team as well, as they will know their assets the best.

It should be noted at this point that the terms "Cyber Reviews" and "Cyber Assessments" are very often used synonymously with the term of "Cyber Audit". This is far from what reality dictates. Each of these processes have their own distinct purposes and objectives of what needs to get accomplished, and with regard to the Cyber Audit, one of the other primary objectives is to make sure that the Controls that have been deployed and implemented are actually certified and do come into compliance with the many legislations and regulations that are in existence, most notably those of the GDPR, CCPA, and HIPAA. These topics are the focal point of Chapter 4 of this book.

In the Audit process, there are typically four distinct parties that are involved, and are as follows:

1) The Auditee
   This is the company that is actually the subject of the Cyber Audit.

2) The Lead Auditor
   This is the person who is leading the Cyber Audit. If it is being done internally, it will be the CISO, or if it is being done by an external third party, then this person is typically known as the "Lead Auditor". If a mixture of both teams are being used, then it will be both the CISO and the Lead Auditor that will be in charge.

3) The Auditor
   This is the team of individuals that will actually be carrying out the Cyber Audit functions and activities. In this regard, it will be the IT Security team, or the team that reports to the Lead Auditor if an external, third party is utilized. A combination of both teams can be used as well.

4) The Client
   This is the organization that will be experiencing the Cyber Audit.

Why the Cyber Audit Is Conducted

There are many reasons why a Cyber Audit is conducted. Typically, as previously reviewed in this chapter, it is to determine where the vulnerabilities and the weaknesses lie within both the physical- and digital-based assets, and to come up with a proper plan of action in order to determine which types and kinds of Controls will work best to remediate them to the greatest extent possible (as overcoming them 100% is not feasibly or realistically possible).

But there are other reasons as well and they typically include the following:

- A regulatory agency may require it in order to make sure that the company in question is in full compliance with the provisions and statutes that have been set forth by the likes of the GDPR, CCPA, HIPAA, etc.
- A follow-up Cyber Audit may often be needed because the previous one revealed serious Cyber-related issues that needed and required prompt attention. Thus, the primary purpose of the follow-up Cyber Audit is to make sure that all of these issues have been addressed and resolved.
- It could also very well be the case that carrying out a Cyber Audit is an activity that is deemed to be an ongoing one, as dictated by the Security Policy of the company in question.

It should be noted at this point that although the reasons may vary as to why a Cyber Audit is needed, the theoretical aspects that underpin the fundamentals of it are often found in a specified type or kind of Framework. These are typically the ones that are found with the National Institute of Standards and Technology (also known as "NIST"), the COBIT, ISO 27000, NIST 800-53, NIST 800-172 (this is primarily used for the Cybersecurity Maturity Model Certification, also known as the "CMMC"), etc.

These are all formalized Accounting and Control-based Frameworks. Thus, before an actual Cyber Audit can even be conducted, it is very important for the CISO and their IT Security team to decide which of these Frameworks are most applicable to their company, and from there, follow the specific tenets and provisions that reside within them. These Frameworks are available as public documents and can be downloaded by conducting a Google-based search for the appropriate Framework.

As also mentioned earlier in this chapter, the actual process by which the Cyber Audit is carried out is a direct function of the company in question, and what their own unique Cybersecurity requirements are. As a result, these Frameworks, apart from containing their tenets and provisions describing how the Cyber Audit should be conducted (in general terms), also consist of a series of Templates that help further guide the CISO and their IT Security team as to how they will carry out, conduct, and execute their Cyber Audit.

These Templates can also be used to meet the following criterion:

- Any industry or market sector standards and best practices that are relevant to the company that is conducting the Cyber Audit;
- Helping to determine and further ascertain any platform-based elements that have not been previously specified;
- Formulate, develop, and execute a set of plans that will detail the types and kinds of Controls that will be used to remediate the weaknesses and vulnerabilities that are found in the physical- and digital-based assets. Further, this document of the set of plans will also consist of the following:
  - Clearly and succinctly identify those specific physical- and digital-based assets that will need the Controls;
  - A system for concretely evaluating the effectiveness of the Controls that are to be deployed and implemented;
  - How additional compliance checks will be established and used to make sure that the Controls are indeed working effectively over a pre-established time period;
  - As mentioned earlier in this chapter, conduct further Cyber Audits as a means to further test the Controls that have been implemented.

Remember that one of the other primary objectives of conducting the Cyber Audit is to convince the other members of the C-Suite and the Board of Directors that ultimately in the end, all of the needed steps are being taken to bring down the overall level of Cyber Risk that a company is facing, by also making use of the right set of Controls.

A good rule of thumb here for the CISO and their IT Security team is that before even deciding what kind or type of Cyber Audit Framework should be utilized, it may be first necessary to just conduct a very general, high-level Cyber Audit first to see what exactly the situation is that the company is facing. It is important to keep in mind that this will be a very much toned down version of the actual Cyber Audit that will subsequently be devoted to it. Thus, the time that is required to do this task should also in turn be substantially reduced.

The Principles of Control in the Cyber Audit

Although one of the primary objectives of the Cyber Audit is to see where the vulnerabilities and weaknesses of both the physical and digital assets lie, one of the others (which is obviously the next step) is for the CISO and their IT Security team to take a proactive mindset to determine which Controls will be needed. By taking this kind of unique approach, the selection, procurement, and deployment of these Controls will thus be in a much more efficient and effective manner once the Cyber Audit of both the physical and digital assets have been completed.

Keep in mind that determining all of this is at the crux and heart of conducting any type or kind of Cyber Audit. As such, keeping this proactive mindset about the needed Controls can be fostered by making use of these four guiding principles:

- Determining and ascertaining the desired level of outcome and subsequent performance level for the needed Controls;
- Developing a process for further evaluating their performance at a subsequent point in time;
- The ability for the Audit team to compare the results of the Cyber Audit to the operational effectiveness of the Controls that are being seriously considered;
- How to correct and rectify any type or kind of mismatches that could very well occur in the third principle; in other words, if the results of the Cyber Audit do not conform to the effectiveness of the Controls and vice versa.

During the Cyber Audit, it is very important that there is a high level of responsibility that is associated with each process that is going on.

Any sort of documentation that transpires in this process must also be very clear and succinct so that anybody involved can understand what is going on. In other words, the Audit team (whether it is internal or externally based) should never stray away from the Templates that resides from within the documentation of the Framework that is ultimately chosen.

From these particular Templates, the roles as well as the responsibilities of the members of the Audit team must be specifically spelled out, so that there is no cross-over of duties (especially in the duplication of work-related activities). In this regard, if there is any deviation, it must also be spelled out as to what exactly comprises it. For instance, will there be any allowance for the Audit team members to help each other out in case a member (or even members) become incapacitated to do their work? These are some of the key issues that need to be decided upon.

Also, in an effort to determine how the plans should be established in deciding what kind and type of Controls will be needed after the Cyber Audit is over, certain pieces of evidence need to be collected by the Audit team in order to support that effort. In particular, here is what they will be looking for:

- Any existing process that is already related to the physical and digital assets of the organization need to be well documented;
- What their current level of functionality is;
- What the current levels of responsibility are (as well as accountability) for those physical-and digital-based assets. In other words, who is monitoring the existing set of Controls that are in place to make sure that they are supposed to function as they are currently supposed to, in the absence of the new Controls that will be implemented?
- Any other competing Controls that are currently in place. In other words, is one Control being used to help monitor two or more physical- or digital-based assets? If so, is this further eroding its present state of effectiveness.

It is important to keep in mind that although one of the primary objectives of the Cyber Audit is exactly pinpointing the weaknesses and vulnerabilities of the both the physical- and digital-based assets that are currently in place, one of the other key objectives of Cyber

Audit is to also do the same type of examination of the Controls that are currently in place, and anything that is indirectly related to them.

In this particular context, the following are also considered to be Controls and will be further examined as the Cyber Audit unfolds and transpires.

1) The Data

These are the datasets that are deemed to be internal or external to the company that is the subject of a Cyber Audit. It is important to note that this includes all forms of data, whether it is quantitative or qualitative in nature. One of the typical examples of this are the Personal Identifiable Information (PII) datasets, especially as they relate to both employees and customers.

2) All of the Application Systems

It is important to note that these are not the IT-related applications that a company uses internally or makes externally available to its customers. Rather, it is the summation of both the manual-based and automatic processes that typically run these applications in question.

3) The Technological Aspects

This includes all of the related support software and hardware that are used to run the applications both internally and externally from within the company. Typical examples of this include any sort of Operating Systems (such as those of the Android, iOS, Linux, MacOS, Windows, etc.), any Networking mediums (such as those of Firewalls, Network Intrusion Devices, Routers, etc.), and the relevant Database Management Systems (this includes both Open Sourced and Closed Source applications such as Oracle, SQL Server, MySQL, PostGRE SQL, etc.).

4) The Facilities

These are all of the resources that are involved to house the Controls that support the daily functionalities of both the physical- and digital-based assets. A good example of this is the Data Center which contains all of this.

5) The People

This can be considered to be one of the most critical aspects of any Control that is currently implemented at a business that is the subject of a Cyber Audit, especially those that are involved in running them. Probably one of the best examples of this are the Accounting and IT Departments of the company.

Also, the Audit team should keep in mind that whatever Audit Framework is ultimately chosen, the Templates that reside from within them will consist of a set of high-level objectives and even the structure as to how the Controls should be further classified both in terms of their current usage and levels of effectiveness. In terms of the high-level objectives, there are three of them, and they are as follows:

1) The Operational Objectives

These can be typically viewed as the requirements and criteria that are deemed to be "discrete" in nature. This includes daily processes that are in place in order for the business to serve its industry and the customers according to their Business Plan that has been set forth and established.

2) The Managerial Objectives

These objectives are claimed to be a level up above of the Operational Objectives. This typically involves the IT Department and the IT Security staff. Note that not everybody here may not be explicitly involved at this level; only those individuals that have interrelated activities will actually be involved in this part of the Cyber Audit. A typical example of this is the Network Administrator who is also involved with Network security-related activities.

3) The Organizational Objectives

This particular domain is deemed to be at a level that is higher up than the Managerial Objectives. This once again typically relates to the IT Department and even the IT Security team, in general. For example, these are the specific functionalities that are typically involved for these two departments to run smoothly and effectively as well as the work outputs that are produced that can have a cascading style of impact upon other areas of the company currently undergoing the Cyber Audit.

In terms of the Classification Structure, these can be further grouped into procedural realms which are as follows:

1) <u>The Specific Strategies That Relate to the Company</u>
   These are the places in the business entity in which the Security Policies and the Audit Frameworks are the *most relevant*. Further, this area is primarily concerned with as to how both of these mechanisms can make a meaningful contribution to the overall Cybersecurity growth of the company in question.

2) <u>The Development and the Application Environments</u>
   This is where the Security Policies and the Audit Frameworks will be *deployed and implemented* at the place of business. This area is chiefly concerned with turning these two mechanisms into both measurable and quantifiable actions and steps.

3) <u>The Enterprise Sustainment Environment</u>
   This is where the Security Policies and the Audit Frameworks will be *maintained* at the place of business. This is the area in which these two mechanisms will actually be delivered to the company.

4) <u>The Assessment and Management Environment</u>
   These are the people in the key areas of the business who take into account and establishe key decision-making policies based on outputs calculated based on both the Security Policies and the Audit Frameworks. This area is primarily concerned with the operational monitoring and review processes of these two mechanisms just described.

The Validation of the Audit Frameworks

As it has been demonstrated from the previous subsections of this chapter, the selection of the Audit Framework is one of the most important components to take into consideration by the CISO and their IT Security team. After all, the Templates that reside in them will further dictate as to how the actual Cyber Audit will take place, and from there, the needed Controls will be selected, procured, and deployed. Then from that point, these newly implemented Controls will then be continuously monitored on a real-time basis in order further ensure that they are working and operating at the peak, optimal levels that they are supposed to.

Thus, as one can see, the selection of the appropriate Audit Framework can have a serious, cascading effect, either positive or negative, for the entire Cyber Audit Cycle. Thus, it is absolutely imperative that the CISO and their IT Security team make sure that the chosen Audit Framework has been validated and tested so that its conformity exactly meets the security requirements of the business that is going through the steps of the Cyber Audit.

This Validation Process consists of four different phases, and on a very high level, they are deemed to be as follows:

- How the exact specifications of the chosen Audit Framework fits into the IT processes of the company. In other words, will there be a direct one to match with everything, and if this does not exist, what are the steps that can be taken to achieve this particular level of conformity?
- How the exact requirements, goals, and objectives of the Cyber Audit will meet the specifications of the Audit Framework itself. In a way, this can be viewed as the opposite of the last step just reviewed. For example, if the needs of what is to be accomplished from the Cyber Audit cannot be met by the specifications that are set forth by the selected Audit Framework, how can this bridge be gapped, so that the Audit itself can be initiated and completed on a timely basis?
- How will the processes for each Control already in place be met by the specifications that have been set forth by the specifications in the chosen Cyber Framework? In other words, will the Templates that are provided in the related documentation be enough to conduct a thorough and exhaustive Audit of the processes that are currently in existence for each and every established digital and physical asset that reside in the IT and Network Infrastructure? If this cannot happen, how can it be made so that there will be a perfect match between the specifications and the processes? Will the templates that are provided in the relevant documentation be further modified?
- As previously mentioned, each Audit Framework has its own set of specifications. Another area of concern before the exact

Audit Framework can be validated is if these specifications that have been established and set forth match with the principles and reasoning as to why that particular Control has been bee deployed and installed in the first place. If there is not a perfect match in this regard, how can this be achieved before the actual Cyber Audit can take place?

A Macro View of How the Cyber Audit Process Works

At this point in this chapter, it is very important to note that the Cyber Audit process is actually a very highly disciplined approach, and one that should be taken very seriously by the CISO and their IT Security team, as there is a lot that is at stake, especially from the standpoint of bringing down the level of Cyber Risk where the organization is currently at. In fact, although the heart of the Cyber Audit is to determine what kinds and types of Controls are needed, the Cyber Audit and the procurement and the deployment of the necessary Controls are done in two very different and succinct phases. Typically, it is the former that is done first, then the latter.

In this subsection of this chapter, we provide a macro view, or an overview, as to how the Cyber Audit actually takes place. But to start off with first, apart from ascertaining the weaknesses and the vulnerabilities of both the physical- and digital-based assets and determining the needed Controls for them, one of the other main objectives of conducting a Cyber Audit is to not only instill a sense of accountability to the CISO and their IT Security team, but also developing the strategies and techniques to keep this sense of accountability moving on a real-time basis.

Therefore, the main processes of the Cyber Audit can be highlighted as follows:

- The identification of all of the significant physical- and digital-based assets that comprise the IT and Network Infrastructure;
- The documentation of all of the designs of the Controls that have already been implemented and which are currently in place;
- The actual evaluation of the designs of these Controls;
- The examination of the particular effectiveness of these already-established Controls;

- The weaknesses and the vulnerabilities of these Controls and how they can be remediated so that they still be functionable going forward after the Cyber Audit has been completed and the new Controls (if they are needed) have been put into place;
- The documentation of how all Controls, whether they are already established or new, will be examined for their effectiveness and optimization going subsequently into the future.

When the Cyber Audit is first triggered, the pinpointed areas of what needs to be studied are first given a careful examination and all of the relevant documentation that is associated with them. If the documentation in hand already appears to be sufficient enough, then there may not be a need to further conduct the Cyber Audit. But, this is a call that is to be made by the CISO and their IT Security team. But, on the other hand, if the documentation that is already in hand appears to be lacking in any way, shape, or form, then most likely, the Cyber Audit will continue.

Keep in mind that conducting a Cyber Audit, especially if it is a full blown one, can be not only a very time-consuming one, but a very expensive one as well, especially for the organization that is going to be the target of it. But in the end, if it is decided that the Cyber Audit must continue, then the first steps are to collect the needed pieces of evidence to further substantiate that the documentation already in hand is lacking. This is actually done by collecting the needed evidence from the following sources:

- The interviewing of the relevant employees of the organization who have had a particular role in the formulation of the documentation that is relevant to the Controls that have already been deployed;
- The thorough examination of the existing documentation to see specifically where the inadequacies lie;
- The review of any types or kinds of manuals that are associated with the already-established set of Controls;
- The careful studying and examination of the analysis of the information that resides in these pieces of documentation;

- The careful observation of the workflows of the employees that are closely associated with the Controls that are already put into place, as well as taking careful note of the environments that they are presently working in.

This not at all by any means an inclusive list, but it is at least a very good starting point for the CISO and their IT Security team. But, once the above-mentioned process has been completed, all pieces of evidence that have been collected are further discussed, especially from the standpoint of the discrepancies that have been unearthed. This then provides the foundation for conducting the Risk Analysis phase of the Cyber Audit. As also reviewed previously, this part involves the very careful inventorying of both the physical- and digital-based and ranking them on a scale as posing the greatest vulnerability to the lowest level of vulnerability.

The Importance of Cyber Audit Management

As one can see throughout this entire chapter thus far, conducting the actual Cyber Audit is a very complex process with a lot of moving parts to it. So, it is highly advisable that there is a separate Audit Management function to oversee all of this, and it should not be by any means the CISO or any members of the IT Security team (or for that matter, any members from the IT Department) so that there is no skewedness, impartiality, or a sense of biasness that can be introduced at this point in the process.

In general, there are three main areas in which the selected Audit Management will be responsible for, and they are as follows:

1) The Pre-Cyber Audit Phase
   This involves the management of all of the activities that must take place before the actual Cyber Audit. This includes the following steps:
   - Ensuring that the proper planning phases have been completed;
   - Obtaining the actual written permissions and/or approvals in order to launch and execute the actual Cyber Audit;
   - Providing a backup for the information and data that has been collected in the documentation as previously described;

- Maintaining an oversight by reporting any problems that have been encountered and dealt with thus far in the process;
- The formulation of any initial or preliminary conclusions;
- The likewise formulation of any subsequent actions that need to be taken by the CISO and their IT Security team.

2) The Management of the Cyber Audit Team Members

Once it has been decided what the formal Cyber Audit process is, then the actual Cyber Audit team needs to be assembled and given their tasks and responsibilities of what needs to get done. But more importantly, the Cyber Audit Management team needs to make sure that the chosen team has the necessary breadth and depth of Cyber Auditing experience in order to carry out this part of the process. More specifically, the Cyber Audit Management team should be on the lookout for the following:

- A thorough understanding of the standards and best practices that have to be deployed, implemented, and followed through on;
- Have a thorough understanding of the physical- and digital-based assets of the organization that is the target of the Cyber Audit;
- Have an good knowledge of all of the application regulatory laws and key pieces of legislation that apply to the first two; typically, this will be the likes of the GDPR, the CCPA, the HIPAA, etc.;
- Have the necessary skillsets that are required to carry out the actual steps and processes of the Cyber Audit, especially in their experiences and the relevant certifications that they possess. These skillsets are mandatory from both a technical and professional standpoint;
- Have enough requisite training to carry out the actual Cyber Audit.

3) The Management of the Actual Cyber Audit Process Itself

In addition to the two main management functions just mentioned, the Cyber Audit Management team has the following responsibilities as well to conduct the Cyber Audit Process once it has been launched and executed:

- Making sure that the members of the Cyber Audit team maintain a very strong sense of ethics, responsibility, and accountability throughout the entire Cyber Audit Lifecycle;

- Maintaining a review period in which each Cyber Auditor's job role and performance are carefully evaluated on a regular basis;
- Making sure that a sense of consistency and uniformity has been set forth and is being observed by the Cyber Audit team members (this is especially crucial when examining the key pieces before the actual Cyber Audit is conducted as previously reviewed in this chapter);
- The creation, planning, scheduling, and implementation of all of the Cyber Audit activities;
- Establishing a set of best standards and practices as it relates to the reporting of the results of the Cyber Audit (in other words, there should not be too many disparaging differences when the Cyber Audit comes out with their final results);
- The careful monitoring of the transition to the post-Cyber Audit activities, which in most cases is the selection, procurement, deployment, and implementation of the needed Controls to remediate the weaknesses and vulnerabilities of both the physical- and digital-based assets that have been discovered as a result of the Cyber Audit;
- Making sure that all documentation and findings of the Cyber Audit remain in an ultra-secure area. This also means making sure that only certain individuals have access to this and that the integrity of all document pieces are maintained to the highest degree possible;
- More importantly, making sure that all members of the Cyber Audit team have all of the necessary tools and resources in which a fair, objective, and totally unbiased Cyber Audit can transpire from within.

It should also be noted here as well that the Cyber Audit management team maintains a full oversight in terms of the reporting of the deficiencies, especially as it relates to the Controls. This means that nothing should be hidden and each and every deficiency must reported in full in the final report in order to warrant the full justification of conducting the actual Cyber Audit in the first place.

In this regard, there are two main types of deficiencies as they relate to the Controls:

1) The Design Deficiencies

   These happen when a particular Control or a set of Controls is operating at within prescribed parameters, but the output that they are yielding is not totally optimal yet.

2) The Operating Deficiencies

   In this situation, there are two subsets:

   - The Significant Weakness

     This is where a deficiency in one or more Controls could have a cascading effect of failure upon the rest of the Controls that have been deployed and implemented throughout the business in question.

   - The Material Weakness

     This is where the Controls could potentially have deficiencies that reside within them. So, given this fact, one of the other objectives of the Cyber Audit is to not only detect the vulnerabilities that exist in the physical and digital assets, but also the Controls that protect them.

Finally, compliance is a term that is often bandied about conducting a Cyber Audit. For the purposes of clarity, the term compliance refers when the already existing set of Controls or the new set of Controls is meeting the stringent requirements as set forth by such key pieces of legislation as HIPAA, the GDPR, the CCPA, etc.

A Holistic View of How the Cyber Audit Process Works

The last subsection of this chapter provided an overview as to how the entire Cyber Audit looks like and what is exactly entailed in the entire process. In this subsection of this chapter, we will now dive much deeper as to how the Cyber Audit Process is conducted, but this time, filling in much more of details. It is important to keep in mind that conducting a Cyber Audit is implementing a series of intricate, detailed, and complex steps. It is not thrown together all at the last minute; rather it can take months to plan out the entire process.

To recap, the very first step that is involved in the Cyber Audit Process is for the CISO and their IT Security team to truly determine what the real scope of the Cyber Audit is. Although it will be primarily about finding and discovering the weaknesses and vulnerabilities of the physical- and digital-based assets, there could be other objectives as well that still have yet to be ascertained. From here, the next step is to further refine not only the scope of the Cyber Audit Process, but to also determine what some of the information requirements are.

This will of course start with the document process as it was discussed earlier in this chapter, and this will also include determining the following requirements:

- Any recent changes that have transpired which could have an impact upon the business especially as it relates to its IT and Network Infrastructure;
- Any recent changes from within the IT and Network Infrastructure itself;
- Anything that may have recently impacted the IT and Network Infrastructure, which could thus have had a cascading effect on the Controls that have already been put in place;
- How the Controls that are already in existence are overseen and maintained currently by the CISO and their IT Security team;
- Any other related Cyber Audits that may have been conducted prior to the one about to be launched and executed;
- Any outcomes of any other tests that may have been conducted to the physical and digital assets that reside from within the IT and Network Infrastructure.

As it also has been described earlier in this chapter, the entire scope and strategy of the Cyber Audit on what the requirements of it will exactly entail. Once again, it will be a key area for the Cyber Audit management team to determine, deploy, and implement processes for the teams that are conducting the Cyber Audit to follow in a diligent, responsible, and timely manner. The CISO and their IT Security team need to follow up on the following key areas as well:

- What the nature and scope of the overall Cyber Audit is;
- Formally ascertaining all of the processes (both internal and external) that will be part of the Cyber Audit Process;

- The interoperability of all these individual processes and how they work together as a cohesive unit;
- The definition of all of the roles and responsibilities of each and every individual who will be involved in the Cyber Audit. This even includes holding them responsible and accountable for all of their work and actions that transpire throughout the lifecycle of the entire Cyber Audit Process;
- The determination of any informational requirements (this will primarily be once again the documentation);
- The determination of any known Cyber Risks as it relates to the physical and digital assets;
- The determination and confirmation of any changes and the results of those changes that have transpired in the process flows that are found within the IT and Network Infrastructure;
- The determination of any Controls that have may been used prior to the ones that are already in existence and being used;
- Making a further determination of those processes that need to be closely examined in the next Cyber Audit that is about to be launched and executed;
- The ascertaining of any type or kind of architecture that is associated (even in the most remote sense) with the processes that correlate with the IT and Network Infrastructure;
- The allocation and utilization of any and all resources that are to be used in the Cyber Audit Process;
- The formulation and execution of the appropriate Cyber Audit strategies;
- The categorization of the Controls that are already in place or currently being used according to their level of vulnerability and/or weakness. This will be conducted in a way that is very similar as it was done for the physical and digital assets at the beginning of the Cyber Audit.

As it was also described earlier in this chapter, the purpose and scope of a Cyber Audit are not just to discover the weaknesses and the vulnerabilities that exist in the physical- and digital-based assets. It is also to determine the vulnerabilities and the weaknesses in the Controls that have been deployed and implemented to secure them. Thus, in this regard, there are four general steps in to be followed in the Cyber Audit Process when it comes to the examination of the Controls that are already in place. These steps include the following:

1) The determination of how the current system of Controls are working, from both an efficiency and optimizing standpoint;
2) Determining what actually is transpiring and occurring in the Controls that are currently in place;
3) The comparison of the efficiencies of the Controls that are already in place to what the baseline standards currently are at;
4) If there is a mismatch between these two, how can it be justified and further resolved.

In the documentation phase of the Cyber Audit Phase that specifically involves the thorough and exhaustive understanding of how the existing Controls are already working, the following are mandatory items that must be noted by the CISO and their IT Security team:

1) The requirements of the Controls that have already been put into place;
2) How they are organized from in the IT and Network Infrastructure that houses them;
3) The specific and explicit responsibilities and roles of the individuals who are tasked in this part of the Cyber Audit Process;
4) Any and/or all of the statutes of the GDPR, the CCPA, HIPAA, etc., that relate to the compliance section of these Controls;
5) The measures, KPIs, and other types and kinds of metrics that have been put into place to specifically measure and monitor the operational effectiveness of the Controls;
6) Any reporting mechanisms that are being used to frame the output of the key findings and results when the time comes to compile and produce the final report to the Cyber Audit management team.

One of the key questions that is asked at this point is how does one actually measure the effectiveness and optimization levels of the Controls prior to the Cyber Audit to be launched and executed.

This can be based for the most part, on a macro level, upon the following variables:

- The determination and documentation of any processes which exist at the current time as they relate to the Controls that are going to be examined in the Cyber Audit;
- If there are actually any deliverables that exist from within these existing set of Controls;
- Where the backup (technically known as the "Compensating Controls") exist. These are put into action if any of the other primary Controls have failed for whatever reason;
- How far, or to what specific degree the already set of established Controls are meeting their specific objectives. This part will further require a new set of procedures to be established by the Cyber Audit management team, which will involve the tasks of collecting more evidence, especially from the standpoint of documentation.

One of the final steps in this entire process is to alert both the C-Suite and the Board of Directors as to how these existing set of Controls are working, and if they are actually bringing down the level of risk that the company is currently facing. This can be achieved by the following tasks:

- The proper and formal documentation of the vulnerabilities and weaknesses of the current set of Controls that have already been deployed and implemented;
- The determination of how these vulnerabilities and weaknesses can be further taken advantage of in the case of a Cyberattack or major security breach;
- Providing enough detailed information in which various cross-comparisons can be made, for example, comparing the actual results that have been calculated to what their baseline efficiencies and optimization levels should be at.

Finally, it should be noted that these three steps should be reported in the clearest and most concise way possible to the C-Suite and the Board of Directors. If this is done properly and accurately, then the chances are much greater that the CISO and the IT Security team to do very well and get the increase in budget and funding that they need so desperately in today's economic times, which is being severely impacted upon by the COVID-19 pandemic.

A Review of the Cyber Audit Frameworks

So far in this chapter, we have reviewed in some rather extensive detail the Cyber Audit Process that takes place. It is very important to note at this point that whatever has been covered thus in far in this aspect is by no means an exhaustive review. There are many aspects that can go with it, once again, a lot of this depends primarily upon how large the organization is, what their IT Security requirements are, and most importantly, what their specific objectives are when it comes to launching and executing a full-scale Cyber Audit. As mentioned previously in this chapter, conducting a Cyber Audit can be a very expensive and extremely time-consuming process for all parties that are involved with it.

Therefore, it should not be taken lightly and the reasons for doing it must be quite compelling. But there are of course other reasons why a Cyber Audit needs to be conducted, and in these particular cases, it is because the company or organization in question has not come into full compliance with the likes of the GDPR, the CCPA, HIPAA, etc. In these cases, a Cyber Audit is mandatory so that any issues can be quickly remediated before any steep financial penalties are thus imposed.

As it has been examined thus far in this chapter, at the heart of conducting any Cyber Audit is the specific Framework from which it specifically originates from. These are actual pieces of documentation, which spell out the best standards and practices for the Cyber Audit to be carried out. They also contain the needed Templates with which to carry out these specific Cyber Audits. Therefore, in this part of this chapter, we do a deeper dive into all of these specific Frameworks. Subsequently, we will do a technical review of all of the specific Controls that are associated with them.

Breaking Down the Importance of Information Technology (IT) Security Governance

The actual realm of these various types and kinds of Frameworks actually arises from the philosophies that have been set forth by an organization known as the "Information Systems Audit and Control Association" or "ISACA" for short. These tenets are as follows:

1) <u>The Strategic Alignment of the Company</u>

   This is where the Cybersecurity activities of the organization in question must be very closely aligned and also be parallel with the business objectives and processes. Some of the specific variables that are taken into serious consideration here include the following:
   - The style of Cybersecurity Governance:
   - The culture of the company;
   - The hierarchical structure of the company;
   - All of the physical and digital assets that have been deployed.

2) <u>The Cyber Risk Management Profile</u>

   This is the specific level of Cyber Risk that the company is at in a particular point in time, and from there, calculating the particular level of "Residual Cyber Risk" that is there (this is a concept that was also covered previously in Chapter 1).

3) <u>The Business Management Process</u>

   This is the unified cohesion of all of the processes in the business that must come together to further enhance the lines of defenses for the company in question.

4) <u>The Resource Management Function</u>

   This is where the CISO and their IT Security team all come together to make sure that there is an efficient and effective means of Resource Allocation from within the company in order to further enhance their specific level of Security Posture.

5) <u>The Level of Performance Management</u>

   This is the set of IT and Cybersecurity processes that are closely aligned and in parallel with the business processes of the organization. This typically involves constant examination of what exactly is proliferating in the Cyber Threat Landscape for that particular company.

6) <u>The Integration Functionality</u>

   This is the part of the ISACA documentation that confirms that all of the processes of the business, both from a technical and nontechnical perspective, work together in a cohesive fashion, as one holistic unit, from an end-to-end standpoint.

In the next subsection, we now examine in greater detail the Cyber Frameworks.

A Deep Dive into the Cybersecurity Frameworks

Before we do a detailed, technical review of all of the Cyber Frameworks, it is first very important to summarize them, which is depicted in Table 2.1.

Table 2.1 The Various Cybersecurity Frameworks

THE FRAMEWORK	THE SPECIALIZATION	THE ORGANIZATION THAT SPONSORS IT
The COSO	Financial Management/Risk Management	The Committee of Sponsoring Organizations (COSO)
The ITIL	Best practices and guidelines for the management of IT and related Cyber services	The Information Technology Infrastructure Library (ITIL)
The ISO	This is an international organization that focuses upon the following: • IT Service Management; • IT and Cybersecurity Management; • The Corporate Governance of both IT Security and Cybersecurity; • IT Security and Cybersecurity Risk Management; • Quality Assurance (QA) Management	The International Organization for Standardization (ISO)
The COBIT	This is an international organization that focuses on the following: • International-based IT Security and Cybersecurity Governance; • The management of IT Security and Cybersecurity Governance programs; • Providing a listing of best standards and practices for both IT Security and Cybersecurity Risk Management Processes.	The Information Systems Audit and Control Association (ISACA)
The NIST	This is an organization that sets forth both the IT Security and Cybersecurity standards and best practices, that is mandated and further regulated by the Federal Information Security Management Act (also known specifically as "FISMA")	The National Institute of Standards and Technology (NIST)

(Continued)

Table 2.1 (Continued)

THE FRAMEWORK	THE SPECIALIZATION	THE ORGANIZATION THAT SPONSORS IT
The CSF	This is a Cyber Framework that focuses on: • IT Security and Cybersecurity; • The appropriate Risk Management Processes	The Presidential Executive Order 13636, the Improving Critical Infrastructure Cybersecurity
The ISF	This is an international organization that focuses on the following: • IT Security and Cybersecurity Governance; • The management of IT Security and Cybersecurity Risk	The International Security Forum (ISF)
The PCI DSS	This is both an IT Security and Cybersecurity standard for the: • The protection of credit card information and data; • This includes the likes of VISA, Master Card, American Express; and Discover	The Payment Card Industry (PCI) Security Standards Council
The SANS Institute	This is not deemed to be an official Framework, but 20 of the IT Security and Cybersecurity Controls come from the NIST SP 800-53 documentation	The SANS Institute

Source: The Complete Guide To Cybersecurity Risks and Controls: Anne Kohnke, Dan Shoemaker, and Ken Sigler. CRC Press, 2016.

As one can see, a good amount of detail that already exists in Table 2.1 should give you a flavor of what is currently available out there, as well as for the CISO and their IT Security team. Although all of these reviewed Frameworks listed have some sort of bearing on the Cyber Audit Process, the remaining subsections will focus on those Frameworks that not only have the most bearing and impact, but those that also are the most widely utilized by CISOs and their IT Security teams throughout Corporate America.

To start off with, one of the most widely used ones is ISO 27001, which is reviewed in more detail in the next subsection.

The ISO 27001

The ISO entity actually has its roots going all the way back to 1947, and is actually independent and neutral from other Cybersecurity-related Framework organizations. This is also the de facto standard that outlines the specific sets of best practices and guidelines as to the various types of Information Security Management Systems (ISMSs) that need be provisioned, executed, and subsequently maintained.

Here are some of the key historical perspectives behind the ISO 27001:

- It was first launched in the 1990s as the British Standard 7799-2;
- It was then relaunched as ISO Standard 17799 in December 2000;
- It was updated in 2005 as ISO 27001:2005. This updated documentation was well formulated and became known as the "Plan Do Check Act", or the "PDCA", that was geared toward the electromechanical industry;
- The latest of the ISO was published in 2013 by the International Electromechanical Commission and was geared toward the Information Technology needs within that specific industry.

From the ISO 27001, there are have been three brand new subsets that have evolved and are as follows:

- The ISO 27001;
- The ISO 27002;
- The ISO 27005.

It should be noted at this point that it is the ISO 27001:2013 that deals primarily with Information Security and Cybersecurity. In this regard, this documentation is concerned primarily with the following:

- Internal and Stakeholder Cybersecurity Requirements;
- What the specific roles of the CISO should be;
- The specific duties and responsibilities of the IT Security team;
- How to address the issue of Cyber Risk;
- The effective resource allocation of both physical- and digital-based assets to address the issues of Cyber Risk;
- How to create an effective Security Awareness Training Program for employees;
- The monitoring of the performance of the Cyber-related Controls that have been implemented;
- The subsequent monitoring of those Controls on a real-time basis.

Further, the ISO 27001:2013 also details what the exact provisions that an effective Security Plan must consist of and further specifies how this Security Plan should be deployed, implemented, and monitored on a real-time basis for the business in question. From here, it is then the ISO 27002 that then lays out the specific details as to how the needed Controls should be procured, deployed, implemented, and subsequently monitored for the overall levels of effectiveness and optimization.

With regard to the to the ISO 27005, this is the specific set of documentation that deals in more detail as to how the actual Cyber Audit should be carried out. It addresses the following topics:

- The identification of the physical- and digital-based assets;
- The assessment of the weaknesses and vulnerabilities that lie within the physical- and digital-based assets;
- How the needed Controls should be chosen in order to remediate what has been found in the last step;
- How these new Controls should be accepted by the CISO and their IT Security team;
- How any findings of key vulnerabilities and weaknesses should be communicated to both internal and external stakeholders;
- The subsequent monitoring of the effectiveness and optimizing levels of these newly deployed and implemented Controls;
- How any further weaknesses and vulnerabilities that come about after the Cyber Audit should be specifically remediated.

The COBIT 5

Back in the late 1990s (more specifically, 1998), the IT Governance Institute (also known as the "ITGI") was actually formulated by the ISACA as a means to deploy Cyber-related Controls effectively throughout the organization. From here, the "COBIT 5" was then developed and launched in 2012, and this specific Framework consist of five key provisions or tenets, which are as follows:

1) How to Meet the Needs of the Stakeholders
   Whatever Cybersecurity Governance Model has been decided upon, it must meet the needs of both the internal and the external stakeholders. This typically involves the CISO and

their IT Security team and any other individuals who are related or associated with them.

2) Implementing End-to-End Coverage

This simply means that all of the Cybersecurity–related processes and operations must be deployed, implemented, and monitored on a real-time basis from all of the points of origination to the points of destination, and vice versa.

3) The Implementation of Only One Type or Kind of Framework

As far as possible, only one type of Cyber-related Framework should be deployed and implemented in order to reduce any sort of confusion and to also keep the attacked surface to the minimalistic levels that are possible.

4) The Embracement of a Holistic Cyber Model

This should involve the following components or functionalities:

- Principles;
- The Security Policies;
- The Cyber Framework;
- All Cybersecurity-related processes and operations;
- All of the departmental structures that reside within the organization;
- Addressing the specific ethics and behaviors of employees;
- How to effectively "layer in" the Controls that can be used to protect both the physical- and digital-based assets (in this particular case, it would be the PII datasets of both employees and customers).

It is also important to note that the COBIT 5 also consists of what is known as a "Process Reference Model", which serves as an example as to how the business should create, structure, deploy, and implement their relevant Security Policies. Also in this regard, there must be a system of checks and balances that confirm that the Security Policies are not only operating at their peak levels, but are also being enforced.

The COBIT 5 also spells out the specific provisions that draw the lines between Cybersecurity Governance and Cybersecurity Management. This can be specifically defined as follows:

1) The Governance Aspect

This includes five distinct processes:

- Evaluation;

- Direction;
- Monitoring.
2) The Management:
   This includes of four distinct Cyber domains, which are as follows:
   - The Alignment, Planning, and Organization (also known as the "APO");
   - The Building, Acquisition, and Implementation (also known as the "BAI");
   - The Delivery, Service, and Support (also known as the "DSS");
   - The Monitoring, Evaluation, and Assessment (also known as the MEA").

The National Institute of Standards and Technology

This is actually a nonregulatory-based agency, which was founded in 1901 by the United States Federal Government. Although its original intention was to maintain oversight of the nation's physical science-based laboratories (such as primarily those of the Nuclear Facilities), it was further strengthened to address Cybersecurity needs and issues as well. This was done by the enactment and the passage of the Federal Information Security Management Act (also known as the "FISMA") back in 2002.

More specifically, it is the NIST Special Publication (SP) 800-37 that deals specifically with Cybersecurity, which consists of an 8 pronged model, which is depicted in Table 2.2

The Framework for Improving Critical Infrastructure Cybersecurity

This specific Cyber Framework was actually created and launched on February 2013, under the Presidential Executive Order #13636. It should be noted that this is a voluntary kind of Cyber Framework and actually makes use of the existing best practices, standards, and even guidelines in an effort to bring down as much as possible the current level of Cyber Risk that any business is currently facing in any kind or type of industry. It also deals with a topic known as "Cyber Resiliency" which can be found in the NIDT 2014 documentation set.

Table 2.2 The Components of The NIST 800-37 Publication

THE MODEL COMPONENT	DESCRIPTION
Step 1: Categorization	Confidential information and data must be processed, stored, and transmitted via an "Impact Analysis" approach. This can be found in the NIST SP 800-60.
Step 2: The Selection of the Cybersecurity Control Baseline	There are three different types of levels, which are as follows: • Low-Impact; • Moderate-Impact; • High-Impact. The Cyber Controls are further divided as follows: • Management Controls; • Operational Controls; • Technical Controls.
Step 3: The Supplementation of Security Controls	This is the unique customization of the Cybersecurity Controls depending upon the specific needs of the business.
Step 4: The Documentation of the Security Controls	This is a comprehensive set of documentation that provides detailed insights into all of the Cybersecurity Requirements, and all of the Security Controls that are related to them.
Step 5: The Implementation of the Security Controls	This describes in minute detail how the Cybersecurity Controls will be procured and implemented. Any further descriptions at this point should include the following: • A comprehensive review of any type or kind of Planned Inputs; • The expected behavior of the above; • The expected outputs of the above.
Step 6: How to Assess the Security Controls	This is primarily a detailed review of both the optimization and effectiveness of all of the Cybersecurity Controls that have been deployed and implemented.
Step 7: The Authorization of the Security Controls	This includes an assessment of the following: • The IT Security Plan; • The Cybersecurity Controls; • All plans of action that are related the Cybersecurity Controls; • Any Resource Allocation that is needed to make the Cybersecurity Controls operate in a manner that they are intended to.
Step 8: The Monitoring of the Security Controls	This is an ongoing program to further manage, Control, and document all of the intended changes or actual changes from within the Cyber environment of the corporation. This will typically involve the IT and Network Infrastructures.

Source: The Complete Guide To Cybersecurity Risks and Controls: Anne Kohnke, Dan Shoemaker, and Ken Sigler. CRC Press, 2016.

This Cyber Framework actually consists of three major components, and they are as follows:

1) The Framework Core
   This refers to all of the Cybersecurity-related activities and the desired results that are to be produced across all of the functioning departments of an organization. This component also consists of five distinct and unique subcomponents, which are as follows
   • Identification;
   • Protection;
   • Detection;
   • Responsiveness;
   • Recovery.
   These subcomponents are also based upon the NIST 2014 publication and prove as a very valuable starting for both the CISO and their IT Security team's holistic and business centric approach to lowering the overall level of Cyber Risk that a company faces.

2) The Framework Implementation
   This component provides a high-level overview of the Cyber Risk Management Process that a particular firm has undertaken and is thus further subdivided into four distinct Tiers (Tier 1, Tier 2, Tier 3, and Tier 4). This is further exemplified in Table 2.3.

Table 2.3 The Components of the NIST 800-73 Framework

TIER LEVEL	THE IMPLICATIONS
Tier 1	There is no formal Cyber Risk Management Processes in place; but various options are being considered
Tier 2	The Cyber Risk Management Processes have been approved by the C-Suite and Board of Directors
Tier 3	The Cyber Risk Management Processes have been deployed and implemented as formal Security Policies
Tier 4	The Cyber Risk Management Processes that have been deployed and implemented are constantly being revamped and upgraded via lessons learned by conducing regular Cyber Audits

Source: The Complete Guide To Cybersecurity Risks and Controls: Anne Kohnke, Dan Shoemaker, and Ken Sigler. CRC Press, 2016.

3) The Cyber Framework Profiles

These are the specific categories and other types and kinds of profiles that have been created and formulated as a result of adopting and making use this specific Cyber Framework.

The Information Security Forum Standard of Good Practice for Information Security

This Cyber Framework was actually created and formulated by European Security Forum back in 1989. It should be noted that the European Security Forum is both a not-for-profit and independent Cybersecurity-related consortium. What is unique about this entity is that it actively conducts research on a real-time basis for both Cybersecurity and Information Security. It has also further published a new document called the "Standard of Good Practice for Information Security" and it consists of the following four components.

1) The Security Governance

This section deals specifically with the approaches that can be taken into selecting a good Cyber-related Governance Framework.

2) The Security Requirements

This section deals with the following:

- The best practices and standards for a Cyber Risk Assessment Framework;
- The Confidentiality, Integrity, and Availability (aka "CIA") factors that need to be taken into consideration for the Cyber Risk Assessment Framework;
- Any and all of the relevant laws and legislations (which includes the GDPR, the CCPA, the HIPAA, etc.) that are relevant to the Cyber Risk Assessment Framework.

3) The Control Framework

This component actually consists of 20 preselected high-risk areas that encompasses a total of 97 business processes that a business can choose when evaluating their current level of Cyber Risk.

4) The Security Monitoring and Improvement

This component consists of reporting functionalities that include the following:

- Planning;
- How to conduct the Cyber Audit;
- Reporting and Monitoring tools;
- Information Security Risk Reporting;
- How to monitor the Controls so that they are in compliance with the likes of the GDPR, CCPA, HIPAA, etc.

The Payment Card Industry Data Security Standards

Back in 2004, the major credit card companies came together to create this type of Cyber Framework, which is now known as the "PCI-DSS". This is specifically designed to protect the confidential information of the credit card holders across these major brands:

- Visa;
- Master Card;
- American Express;
- Discover;
- American Express;
- The Japan Credit Bureau.

Further any external third party (such as that of PayPal) that is involved with the processing, transmission, and storage of credit card information and data is also bound to by the provisions and tenets that have been set forth by the PCI DSS. These are follows, as demonstrated by Table 2.4

The Cyber Risk Controls

So far in this chapter we have covered in a good amount of detail Cyber Audits and the various types of Cyber Frameworks that are available for the CISO and their IT Security team to use. Once the Cyber Audit has been completed, the next step is to implement those specific Cyber Controls which will not only help to remediate the weaknesses and vulnerabilities that have been discovered in both the physical- and digital-based assets, but to also help bring down the level of Cyber Risk as well that the company is currently facing.

Table 2.4 The Provisions of the PCI DSS Framework

THE PROVISION	TECHNICAL DESCRIPTION
Provision #1	The organization must build and create a secure network. This primarily deals with Firewalls and Routers.
Provision #2	Never rely upon vendor selected security thresholds; these should be custom created and implemented per the unique security requirements which have been set forth and established.
Provision #3	The protection of cardholder data. This includes the retention, storage, and deletion policies, as well as the management of the Encryption tools that are being used in this regard.
Provision #4	The Encryption of card holder information and data as it is being transmitted to all forms of network mediums.
Provision #5	Making use of update and reliable Antivirus/Antimalware software packages.
Provision #6	The maintenance of secure systems and corresponding applications. This also entails the use of a robust Configuration/Change Management Process. This also includes secure software coding practices.
Provision #7	Cardholder information/data is restricted on a Need to Know basis. This is also referred to as a "Least Privilege Policy".
Provision #8	The assignment of a Unique Identifier for each and every individual that has access to cardholder information and data. This should be alphanumeric based.
Provision #9	The restriction of Physical-based Access to cardholder information and data. Typically, this will involve the Data Center and various types and kinds of servers that support it.
Provision #10	The creation, deployment, and implementation of a network access policy, which consists of network-based log reviews and the monitoring of Audit trails.
Provision #11	The regular testing of the security systems and their associated processes. This includes the routing and deployment of both Threat Hunting and Penetration Testing exercises.
Provision #12	The creation, formulation, deployment, and implementation of an airtight Security Policy for the protection of cardholder information and data.

In this regard, there are five primary functions of Cyber Controls, and they can be seen in Table 2.5

As we delve deeper into this topic in this subsection of this chapter, it would be very appropriate to provide a formal definition of just what a Cyber Control is. It can be technically defined as follows:

The safeguards and the countermeasures that are prescribed for the Information Systems or organizations are designed to:

- Protect the Confidentiality, Integrity, and Availability of the Information and the Data that is processed, stored, and transmitted by those systems/organizations;
- To further satisfy a set of defined Security Requirements.[2]

Table 2.5 The Functionalities of Cybersecurity Controls

THE CYBER CONTROL	SPECIFIC FUNCTIONALITY
Identification	To develop an understanding of the needed Controls to help further manage the particular level of Cyber Risk.
Protection	The procurement and deployment of the right mix of Controls to help fortify the lines of defenses that are associated with the IT and Network Infrastructures.
Detection	The procurement and the deployment of the right mix of Cyber Risk tools to alert the CISO and their IT Security team of any suspicious or anomalous behavior that is transpiring.
Responsiveness	How well the CISO and their IT Security team can respond to a Control or set of Cyber Controls after they have been impacted by a security breach.
Recovery	The procurement and the deployment of the right set of Cyber Control plans in order to ensure a vibrant level of Cyber Resiliency after the organization has been impacted by a security breach.

Source: The Complete Guide To Cybersecurity Risks and Controls: Anne Kohnke, Dan Shoemaker, and Ken Sigler. CRC Press, 2016.

There are numerous groupings of Cyber Control categories and the specific Cyber Controls that go along with each of them. These are examined in further detail in the next subsections of this chapter.

The Goal-Based Security Controls

These are the Cyber Controls that are used to meet the overall Cybersecurity needs of the company. These can be seen Table 2.6.

Table 2.6 The Goals of The Cybersecurity Controls

THE CONTROL	FUNCTIONALITY
The Preventative Control	This is designed to prevent a security breach from actually happening.
The Detective Control	These are Controls which permit the CISO and their IT Security team to further investigate any evidence that may have been collected.
The Corrective Control	The goal is to attempt to actually reverse the effects of a security breach.
The Deterrent Control	This Control is designed to discourage people, especially employees, from engaging in the act of launching a security breach. A typical example of this is Insider Attacks.
The Compensating Control	These are backup Controls that should be the primary set of Controls fail for whatever reason.
The Common Control	This is the set of the same type of Controls that are dispersed throughout different regions of the IT Network Infrastructures.

Source: The Complete Guide To Cybersecurity Risks and Controls: Anne Kohnke, Dan Shoemaker, and Ken Sigler. CRC Press, 2016.

The Preventive Controls

These are the set of Controls that in theory would prevent a Cyberattack from happening in the first place. These are given in Table 2.7.

The Detective Controls

As its name implies, this is the group of Controls that allow for the CISO and their IT Security team to further investigate the origins of a Cyberattack after it has transpired. An important consideration here is what is known as "Attribution". This is where attempts are made by the Digital Forensics team to find out that individual or group of individuals specifically responsible for launching that particular threat vector. In this regard, Table 2.8 reviews the Controls that can found and utilized in this specific category.

It should be noted at this point the primary difference between the Detection and Prevention Controls. With the former, these sets of Controls cannot really predict or even make an accurate assessment as to the Cyberattack's potentially goal. Whereas, this is the goal of the latter set of Controls, in which both AI and ML tools are used to

Table 2.7   The Goals of the Cyber Preventative Controls

THE CONTROL	FUNCTIONALITY
The Hardening Control	This is when a particular system in either the IT or Network Infrastructure has more security layers deployed onto it than the default settings call for.
The Security Awareness/ Training	This is much more of a qualitative Control, in that employees are given specialized training in how to maintain good levels of what are known as "Cyber Hygiene".
The Security Guard	These are the human beings that maintain strict access and oversight into the primary and secondary entry/exit areas in the physical premises of the business.
The Change Management	This is the Control which keeps track of all the changes that have transpired thus far in the IT and Network Infrastructures. All changes, upgrades, and revisions are thoroughly documented by this set of Controls.
The Account Disablement Control	This is the Control which either automatically terminates or permanently disables all of the accounts of an employee after they have been fired or terminated.

Source: The Complete Guide To Cybersecurity Risks and Controls: Anne Kohnke, Dan Shoemaker, and Ken Sigler. CRC Press, 2016.

Table 2.8 The Goals Of The Cyber Detective Controls

THE CONTROL	FUNCTIONALITY
The Log Monitoring	These are the log files that are created and output by all of the Network Security tools. Prime examples of this include Firewalls, Routers, Network Intrusion Devices, etc.
The Trend Analysis	This is the Control that allows for the CISO and their IT Security team to conduct high-level statistical analyses of the log files in order to track down any suspicious or anomalous behavior.
The Security Audit	These are Controls that can automatically scan a system in the IT and Network Infrastructures in order to determine if Security Policies are being followed by both end users and employees alike.
The Video Surveillance	This Control makes specific usage of Closed Circuit Television Cameras Technology (CCTV) in order to record in real time all activity that transpires from both the internal and external environments of the business.
The Motion Detection	This is the Control that can detect the movement of people if they were to access areas that they are not authorized to enter.

Source: The Complete Guide To Cybersecurity Risks and Controls: Anne Kohnke, Dan Shoemaker, and Ken Sigler. CRC Press, 2016.

get a much better predicament into this, and this alerts the CISO and their IT Security team. Also, it should be noted that Cyber Controls can also be considered as "Hybrid" if they are commonly used across different areas of the IT and Network Infrastructures. There are three distinct advantages to this:

- Making use of Controls in this fashion can help result in substantial cost savings;
- It permits for a much greater flow or degree of consistency across the entire spectrum of the business across all of the assets that they are designed to protect, whether they are physical based or digital based in nature;
- Also, examining a set of common Cyber Controls can result in significant savings in case a Cyber Audit were to be actually conducted. For example, rather than examining the same Cyber Control over and over again in different environments of the IT and Network Infrastructure, only one set of these and only one environment need to be carefully examined.

Table 2.9

THE CONTROL	FUNCTIONALITY
The Vulnerability Assessments	This Control attempts to mitigate the weaknesses and vulnerabilities that lie *within* the IT and Network Infrastructures.
Penetration Testing	This Control attempts to mitigate the weaknesses and vulnerabilities that lie *outside* the IT and Network Infrastructures.
The Contingency Planning	This involves the creation, deployment, and implementation of the Incident Response, Disaster Recovery, and Business Continuity Plans.
The Physical and Environmental Protection	These are the Controls that are used to specifically protect the business from the outside or the external environment.
The Media Protection	These are the Controls set in place to further fortify the security levels of Portable Media Devices. A prime example of this is the USB Flash Drives.

Source: The Complete Guide To Cybersecurity Risks and Controls: Anne Kohnke, Dan Shoemaker, and Ken Sigler. CRC Press, 2016.

The Operational Controls

While there is no doubt that all kinds of Cyber Controls are very important to bring down the particular level of Cyber Risk for the company in question, it is this grouping of Cyber Controls that is deemed to be among the most important. For example, if an organization were to be impacted by a security breach, how quickly can it resume its mission critical processes, and over a period of time, come back to full normalcy? These are all addressed by this category of Cyber Controls, and they are as follows as given in Table 2.9.

Finally in the end, one of the other ultimate objectives of a robust set of Cyber Controls is to protect the lifeblood of any business: The confidential information and data that they store in their databases. There are three groupings of this as well, and they are as follows:

1) Data at Rest
   This can be defined specifically given as follows:

This is the data that is not being accessed and is stored on a physical or logical medium. Examples may be files stored on file servers, records in databases, documents on flash drives, hard disks etc.[3]

In other words, this is the information and data that is not moving anywhere; it is just stationary at one point in time.

2) Data in Transit

This can be defined specifically as follows:

It describes data that is sent over a network (cellular, Wi-Fi, or other networks) or is located in the RAM. At some point, data that was recovered from the device (or data at rest) was also sent over the network.[4]

In other words, this information and data that are actively going across some type or kind of network medium from its point of origination to its final point of destination and any other network node in between.

3) Data in Process

This can be defined specifically as follows

Data processing is the method of collecting raw data and translating it into usable information. It is usually performed in a step-by-step process by a team of data scientists and data engineers in an organization. The raw data is collected, filtered, sorted, processed, analyzed, stored and then presented in a readable format.[5]

In other words, this is the information and data that is being transformed into a usable format so that it is used to meet either the business objectives or scientific objectives of the business entity.

Notes

1 https://securityscorecard.com/blog/best-practices-for-a-cybersecurity-audit
2 NIST Special Publication 800-53: Security and Privacy Controls for Federal Information Systems and Organizations.
3 https://www.sealpath.com/protecting-the-three-states-of-data/
4 https://www.sciencedirect.com/topics/computer-science/data-in-transit
5 https://www.simplilearn.com/what-is-data-processing-article

3
CYBERSECURITY INSURANCE POLICIES

Cybersecurity Risk Insurance Policies

The cybersecurity insurance market is currently volatile due to multiple factors including the prevalence of remote work, cyber-attackers' increased focus on small businesses, and common misconceptions about the purpose and coverage of cybersecurity insurance. The increase in cyber-crime is both a boon and a liability to insurance companies offering coverage for cybersecurity incidents. In the coming years, insurance companies will have to strike a balance between profitability, cyber resiliency, and the appearance of acting in good faith for both their success and for the viability of cybersecurity insurance as a whole.

The State of the Cybersecurity Insurance Market

The cybersecurity insurance market is strong due to the recent increase in cybercrime. Experts predict that the global cybersecurity insurance market will rise to $9.5 billion during 2021, with an estimated 21% growth each year. Experts predict that the cybersecurity insurance market will exceed $20 billion by the end of 2025.[1] A June 2020 survey indicated that six out of ten companies intend to spend more on cybersecurity insurance and that half of those are planning on increasing their investment believing that the cost is worth the coverage.[2]

Recent trends in cyber insurance policy in North America are driven by three factors: the severity and frequency of claims being made, increased efforts by cyber insurance companies to analyze and investigate claims, and the lowering interest rates in North America.[3] These factors lead to two general approaches to generating new leads: lowering prices to undercut competitors and targeting specific target audiences with campaigns that educate and cater to a subset of the customer pool.

DOI: 10.1201/9781003023685-3

Despite the forecasted strength of the overall market, the drawbacks and limitations pertaining to cybersecurity insurance are prominent online and in the media. Common problems within the industry include:

- Cybersecurity policies have gained a reputation for providing inadequate coverage to its policy holders. A study performed by Sophos reveals that only 64% of respondents had coverage for ransomware attacks.[4]
- Encouraging covered clients to pay ransomware attackers could encourage additional ransomware attacks in the future due to the implied incentivization.[5]
- The rising costs of cybersecurity insurance render it virtually impossible for small businesses to acquire as well lead to a significant drain to medium-sized and large businesses.
- The excessive amount of information pertaining to cybersecurity insurance is written either directly by insurance companies themselves or by third-party groups who benefit from cybersecurity insurance sales. Unbiased information regarding cybersecurity insurance is both rare and low-ranking on many search engines.
- Cybersecurity insurance policies have garnered a negative reputation for including exclusionary language. Phrases such as "acts of war" or "targeted attack" allow insurance companies' legal standing to challenge or deny claims that appear to fall within the purchased coverage.
- Cyber insurance companies do not offer coverage for data residing on cloud technology. Insurance companies cannot profit from covering risks associated with data on cloud technology.[6]
- Businesses' tendency to keep negative press buried or to apply spin on adverse events increases the difficulty in gathering and presenting correct data regarding cyber-attacks and the damage that they cause.
- The knowledge gap between the current state of cybersecurity and the lawmakers that regulate cybersecurity insurance could lead to both lack of coverage for vital risks and laws that provide needless restrictions on both cybersecurity insurance providers and their clients.

- Cybersecurity insurance has critics that argue that cybersecurity insurance should not exist at all. In addition to the argument that cybersecurity insurance emboldens cyber-attackers, critics argue that the overall premise of cybersecurity insurance is not profitable, especially as the cost associated with cyber-attacks rises.[7]
- Cybersecurity insurance policy owners may consider cybersecurity insurance as an alternate to strong cyber health instead of its intended purpose. In 2015, Raytheon performed a study on financial services; the study included statistics that argue for the existence of the misuse of cybersecurity insurance:
    - 38% of polled banks at the time of the study encrypted data on their companies' networks.
    - 30% of polled banks did not enforce multifactor authentication for third-party vendors.
    - At least one bank in the Fortune 500 purposefully refrained from applying a software patch that would protect its servers from the Heartbleed bug. The CSO of the bank cited that applying the patch would disrupt operations with their overseas partners who had not yet applied the patch.
    - Even in 2015, both Standard and Poor and AIG expressed concerns that the cost of successful cyber-attacks would outpace the coverage that banks were purchasing, with the highest amount of coverage sold by AIG to a bank in 2015 being $400 million.[8]

Cybersecurity insurance is a relatively new market, separating it distinctly from time-honored insurance products such as auto insurance and home insurance. The state of information pertaining to cybersecurity insurance and cyber-attacks further complicate efforts to define the cybersecurity insurance industry, establish industry-wide standards, and accurately predict the efficacy, long-term ramifications, and long-term profitability of cybersecurity insurance. However, the efforts of many major insurance companies to promote cybersecurity insurance and warn companies of the risks of successful cyber-attacks indicate that enough companies are willing to invest in the industry.

An Analysis of the Major Insurance Carriers That Offer Cyber Insurance

Due to the concentrated public relations efforts of insurance companies and their partners, which companies can be considered significant players in the cybersecurity insurance market, is subject to multiple interpretations, with many sites having conflicting lists and analyses of the best insurance companies. The truth is more nuanced; insurance companies that offer cybersecurity insurance have a combination of coverage levels, services offered, customer outreach, and public images that differentiate themselves from their competitors. An insurance company that sells maximum coverage of $1 million would be a poor choice for a global corporation. Conversely, an insurance company with a minimum coverage of $1 million could be a serious financial drain to small businesses and individual professionals.

The following section is not meant to be an exhaustive list of insurance companies that are active and prominent in the cybersecurity insurance market. These companies either have large market presence, recognizable potential, or a combination of both.

Chubb Limited claims that it is the world's largest publicly traded property and casualty insurance company and commercial insurance provider in the United States. Chubb Limited also sells policies for personal accident and supplemental health, commercial and personal property and casualty insurance, life insurance, and reinsurance. Chubb Limited has $316.3 million in direct premiums written, covering 17% of the cybersecurity insurance market. They have offered coverage for "cyber risk" since 1998.[9]

Chubb Limited's company website postures itself as an all-inclusive provider of cybersecurity services, including its own cybersecurity products and specialized training for client companies. Chubb Limited also provides bulleted lists and tables that describe the incidents covered and advertised benefits of their coverage types. However, Chubb Limited was targeted by a data breach in late March 2020. The ransomware hacking group, Maze, advertised their infiltration of Chubb Limited's network by publishing data that they claim that they stole from Chubb Limited.[10] Chubb claimed that the attack did not impact their IT infrastructure, and follow-up coverage of the aftermath of the attack is slim.

Target Corporation sued Chubb Limited in November 2019 for $138 million over an unpaid insurance claim stemming from Target's data breach incident in 2013. US District Judge Wilhelmina M. Wright ruled in Chubb Limited's favor, citing that Target Corporation did not prove that its expenses associated with distributing new credit card to its clients qualified as "loss of use" as covered by its commercial general liability policies.[11]

Despite complaints pertaining to denial of claims from its other insurance products – including home and auto – Chubb has a strong reputation as a top-quality insurance company. Their high costs make them less than ideal for small businesses and medium-sized businesses, but the range of services that Chubb Limited offers could appeal to large corporations who can afford Chubb Limited's costs far more easily than the costs associated with a cybersecurity attack. Chubb Limited is treated as an overall leader in the insurance industry, though continued negative press regarding its own cyber-attacks and customer service missteps could erode its market share.

American International Group (AIG) sells cyber insurance policies to both businesses and individuals. Its additional products include casualty, accident and health, fronting and captive services, environmental coverage, mergers and acquisitions, management liability, professional liability, political risk, surety, property, and warranty. With $228.7 million in direct premiums written, AIG covers 12.3% of the cybersecurity insurance market. AIG has sold cyber insurance policies for close to 20 years. AIG won the Advisen 2018 Cyber Risk Innovation of the year award for their cybersecurity product, CyberMatics.[12]

SS&C Technologies sued AIG for breach of contract. SS&C lost $5.9 million after a successful spoofing attack from Chinese hackers. The hackers sent emails, posing as one of SS&C Technologies' clients, Tillage Commodities Fund, requesting multiple money transfers to a bank in Hong Kong. AIG claimed that its exclusion of "criminal acts" rendered AIG not liable for SS&C Technologies' insurance claim. AIG's legal team stated that SS&C Technologies affirmed this by describing the funds as "stolen" instead of "lost."[13] US District Judge Rakoff ruled in favor of SS&C Technologies, stating that AIG's policy exclusion did not apply since SS&C Technologies employees believed that the money was being sent to Tillage Commodities Fund, explaining that AIG was "erroneously conflating SS&C's administrative ability to operate Tillage's account, which undisputedly existed, with SS&C's authority and discretionary control over that account."[14]

Though reviews of AIG's cybersecurity services are generally positive, AIG's business tactics have been evidenced as a growing trend among cybersecurity insurance companies to resist paying claims. And AIG has a recent history of scandals including its accounting scandals in 2005 and its prominence in the bailout fiasco in 2008. Though AIG has restored much of its public image, AIG's past can be a liability should similar incidents arise in the future. And its reputation for denying cybersecurity claims may ward off new business, which could be a missed growth opportunity due to the prevalence of cyber-attacks.

AXA XL, the company formed by AXA acquiring the XL group, is a relatively new entrant into the cybersecurity insurance marketplace. In addition to its cyber insurance policies, AXA XL sells casualty, property, specialty, professional and finance, and reinsurance products. Despite winning the distinction of "Highest in Customer Satisfaction among Large Commercial Insurers" in 2017, AXA XL reported a $521.6 million net loss in the same year. Though AXA XL has $177.9 million of direct premiums written and a 9.6% market share, its A.M. Best rating is relatively low at bbb+.[15]

AXA XL does not have significant reputation issues due to a dearth of negative press against it. AXA XL could use this to its advantage with a combination of fortifying an image of honorable business practices and media campaigns that differentiate them from the maligned business practices of their competitors. AXA XL's industry awards can be an asset in both strategies as it prepares itself for the growth in the cybersecurity insurance industry.

Travelers Companies Incorporated is a strong performer in the insurance market; in 2017, Travelers Companies Incorporated reported an approximate $29 billion revenue and nearly $103 billion in total assets. Travelers Companies Incorporated has $119.1 million in direct premiums written, covering 6.4 of the market.[16]

AXIS Capital's insurance products include professional, property and casualty, marine terrorism, credit and political risk, energy, accident, environmental, reinsurance, and health insurance in addition to their cyber insurance policies. In 2017, AXIS Capital reported $5.6 billion in gross premiums and $24.8 billion in total assets. With $101.5 million in direct premiums written, AXIS Capital holds a 5.5% market share.[17]

Beazley Insurance Corporation offers specialized insurance products including political, marine, property, accident and contingency, reinsurance, and property as well as their cyber insurance policies, which the company has offered since 2009. Beazley Insurance Corporation ended the previous decade strong, reporting $2.34 billion in gross premiums and $2.04 billion in revenue in 2017. In 2018, Beazley Insurance Corporation won several industry awards including Launch of the Year, Risk Carrier of the Year, Innovative Initiative, Insurance CEO of the Year, and Insurer of the Year. Beazley Insurance Corporation has $95.0 million in direct premiums written and has a market share of 5.1%.[18]

CNA Financial Corporation focuses on insurance products for professionals and organizations. In 2017, CNA Financial Corporation reported $9.5 billion in revenue and $44.9 billion in total assets. With $73.1 million in direct premiums written, CNA Financial Corporation has a market share of 3.9%. CNA Financial Corporation's cybersecurity insurance focuses on covering breaches in privacy and security.[19]

Blue Cross and Blue Shield is the parent company for BCS Financial Corporation, which was formed over 30 years after Blue Cross and Blue Shield. BCS Financial Corporation reported $622 million in revenue and $1 billion in assets in 2017. In addition to its cyber liability insurance products, BCS Financial Corporation sells ancillary income products, large claim solutions, travel insurance, student accident insurance, agent errors and omissions, and financial solutions such as money market funds. BCS Financial Corporation has written $69.9 million in direct premiums, earning it a 3.8% market share.[20]

AmTrust Financial positions itself to cater to small businesses. AmTrust Financial offers coverage ranging from $50,000 to $1 million, and it does not conduct application processes for coverage limits at or below $100,000. However, AmTrust Financials' outreach and lead generation may be hampered by the company not offering online quotes or standalone coverage for cybersecurity threats.

On June 17, 2020, the SEC charged AmTrust Financial Services and a former Chief Financial Officer, Ronald E. Pipoly Jr., with failure to disclose material facts regarding the company's insurance losses and reserves during the period of March 2010 to February 2016. AmTrust Financial and Ronald E. Pipoly settled the matter out-of-court. AmTrust Financial paid $10.3 million in civil penalties, and Ronald E. Pipoly paid a combined amount of $237,499.[21]

Despite receiving high scores for its customer service from industry blogs and magazines, AmTrust Financial currently receives a high number of customer-submitted negative reviews. AmTrust's financial strength is weak in comparison to its larger competitors as well. It currently remains to be seen whether AmTrust Financial will adjust its practices to attract new leads and improve its image or if the company will maintain its niche status.

The Doctors Company focuses its cybersecurity insurance products for medical businesses and healthcare professionals. In addition to cybersecurity coverage, The Doctors Company sells professional liability insurance, medical malpractice insurance, and workers' compensation coverage. Currently, the Doctors Company is the biggest physician-owned medical malpractice insurer in the United States, claiming 80,000 members and $5.9 billion in assets.

The Hartford Steam Boiler Inspection and Insurance Company focuses its cybersecurity insurance efforts toward small- and medium-sized law firms. Like AmTrust Financial, The Hartford Steam Boiler Inspection and Insurance Company offers low coverage amounts ranging from $50,000 to $1 million.

One common trend among the major players in cyber insurance is the increased emphasis on education and prevention. Unlike some common insurable incidents such as earthquakes and being struck by an at-fault automobile driver, cybersecurity incidents are highly preventable with adequate preventative measures. Insurance companies that train their clients to be more cyber resilient achieve two tangible benefits: they receive positive press associated with their awareness and outreach efforts and they save money by preventing cybersecurity incidents instead of paying for damages – as well as the court fees associated with contesting claims – that result from a successful cybersecurity attack.

The Major Components of a Cyber Insurance Policy

The services offered in cybersecurity insurance can be divided into two categories: first-party coverage which addresses direct loss and damage as a result of the cyber-attack, and third-party coverage, which concentrates on indirect damages and fines.

First-party coverage products include:

- Network security coverage protects companies when their IT network is damaged or rendered inoperable due to malware, data breaches, email compromises, cyber extortion, and ransomware. Network security reimburses direct expenses to the company including IT forensics, legal expenses, data recovery and restoration, ransomware payments, call center operations pertaining to the security incident, notifying clients of the breach, credit monitoring, identity restoration, and public relations.[22]
- Social engineering coverage reimburses expenses associated with psychological manipulation attacks such as phishing, impersonation, and tailgating. Many of the expenses recovered by social engineering coverage involve the quantifiable damage associated with the successful attack, which is in many cases a dollar amount that the attacker accessed after gaining unauthorized access to an account or system. And some insurance companies will offer premium discounts to insured companies that provide cybersecurity awareness training for their employees.[23]
- Notification and breach response coverage reimburses a specific subset of a company's legal fees. When companies hire attorneys to determine the extent to which they need to notify clients and the public after a data breach, notification and breach response coverage pays for the attorney's fees.
- Bricking coverage reimburses companies for IT asset replacement costs. Security incidents that render IT assets non-operational are covered; natural wear-and-tear are typically not covered by bricking coverage.[24]
- Loss or damage to electronic data coverage recovers the costs associated with restoring or replacing electronic data and programs that are stolen, damaged, or destroyed by a cybersecurity incident. This coverage does not differentiate between the company's data, their clients' data, or their partners' data. However, only the cybersecurity incidents specifically covered by the policy will lead to reimbursement. Commonly covered incidents include denial-of-service attacks, computer viruses, and hacker attacks.[25]

- Loss of income and extra expenses coverage reimburses the costs associated with keeping the company open and operational after a specifically covered incident. Certain policies extend coverage to include the lost income and extra expenses dealt to dependents.[26]
- Energy costs associated with cryptojacking – a cyber-attack where hackers install malware on the targets' IT assets to mine digital currencies.
- Operational costs associated with establishing and maintaining a call center to respond to clients of the targeted company.
- Rogue employee coverage, which addresses often-excluded scenarios where a current or former employee of the company instigates the cyber-attack.
- First-party bodily injury and property damage that directly results from the cyber-attack.

Third-party coverage products include:

- Business interruption coverage reimburses companies for the damages associated with the down time between the beginning of a cyber-attack – such as a ransomware attack – and the restoration of the company's IT assets. Some policies cover non-criminal incidents such as a hardware failure or a software update with unintended, catastrophic consequences. Net profit loss is the most common metric used to calculate the reimbursable damages, with insurance policies applying their provisions and formulas to determine the cost of the losses.
- Privacy liability covers expenses associated with the negative consequences and legal violations associated with a data leak. Expenses covered by privacy liability include costs associated with regulatory investigations and liability payments as defined in contracts.[27]
- Media liability covers expenses associated with intellectual property infringement associated with the security breach. Patent infringement is often not covered by media liability coverage.[28]

- Errors and Omissions coverage (more commonly called "E&O coverage") insures companies from expenses associated with the inability of the company to deliver timely, high-quality results to its clients and partners. Expenses covered by Errors and Omissions policies include breach of contract, negligence, indemnification, and defense costs. Though Errors and Omissions coverage applies to technological services, this type of coverage also protects doctors, lawyers, engineers, and architects.[29]
- Reputational harm coverage is a limited-term service that reimburses companies for the expenses that result from the negative public relations following a security incident. Covered expenses include aversion to the company's brand and calculated loss of new leads.
- Third-party bodily injury and property damage resulting from the cyber-attack.
- Reward payments to individuals or groups that supply information leading to the arrest of the cyber-attackers.

Companies should be aware of what damages and expenses are not addressed by cybersecurity insurance. Common expenses not covered by cybersecurity insurance include:

- Legal violations committed by the covered company which contributed to the cyber-attack.
- Failure to adhere to regulations – either external or internal – that could have prevented the cyber-attack.
- Damages associated with the theft of intellectual property.
- Improvement and upgrade costs following a cybersecurity event.
- Potential future lost profits.
- Damage and losses that affect remote workers and workers' personal devices used for work-related activities.
- "Acts of War," which cybersecurity insurance companies use to exclude expenses associated with cyber-attacks from foreign hackers and cyber-attackers.[30]
- Cybersecurity incidents where the affected company is not the "attack target." Cybersecurity insurance policies that employ

"attack target" clauses will only cover attacks that specifically focus on the covered company. This clause allows cybersecurity insurance companies to exclude a variety of social engineering attacks such as phishing and spoofing.[31]

- Increased scrutiny from current and potential investors.
- Declines in market shares.
- Declines in share prices.[32]
- Fraudulent charges on the company's payment cards because of the cyber-attack.
- Damages caused by natural causes including floods, fire, hail, and earthquakes.
- Damages caused by pollution.

Companies should assess their needs and risks, review policies thoroughly, and ask questions directly to the insurance company prior to purchasing coverage.

How Should an SMB Decide on What Kind of Cyber Policy to Get

Though large companies with access to vast amounts of records and resources are prime targets for cyber-attackers, small- and medium-sized businesses are becoming more prominent as targets for hackers and social engineering attacks. As of April 2020, 76% of Northern America's small- and medium-sized businesses faced cyber-attacks.[33] This includes a 57% increase in successful phishing attacks, a 33% increase in stolen devices, and a 30% increase in credential theft. The average cost of a security attack is roughly $141 for each individual stolen or lost record. Even small businesses can face large financial consequences if they store hundreds or thousands of records with sensitive, classified, or confidential records.[34] A study conducted in 2019 reports that 29% of polled customers would not transact with small businesses affected by a data breach.[35] About 60% of small- or medium-sized businesses end up closing their operations completely due to the costs associated with recovering from a cybersecurity event.[36]

The combination of factors that govern companies – including laws, regulations, online presence, technological needs, and urgency of operations – mean that no two companies have the exact same cybersecurity insurance needs. Before seeking quotes for cybersecurity insurance policies, companies should perform an internal assessment of their cybersecurity needs and risks, including:

- Comprehensive, relevant, and up-to-date assessment on the laws, regulations, and procedures that directly and indirectly influence the company's operations.
- The volume and sensitivity of the data that they collect, as well as the crisis recovery plans that will backup and restore company-critical data.
- The estimated costs of the most common types of cyber-attacks, such as security breaches and social engineering attacks.
- The number, quality, and costs of third-party security partners that can assist with recovery from a cybersecurity incident.[37]

The first course of action for small- and medium-sized companies interested in cybersecurity insurance coverage is to conduct a professional network investigation. Cyber risk is like health insurance with respect to whether they cover a potential client – as well as factoring in conditions that may increase or lower annual premiums and the types and limits of coverage offered. Typically, network assessments consider the company's location, size, industry, existing cybersecurity measures, and past cybersecurity incidents.[38]

Small- and medium-sized companies should consider the deductible size of the coverages they purchase. The common deductible for $1 million in coverage is $10,000, with the average annual premium being $1,500 per year.[39] As is the case with other insurance policy products, higher deductibles lead to lower premiums and lower deductibles increase the annual premiums. Small- and medium-sized companies must find the best balance of deductibles, coverages, and premiums that provide cost-effective coverage.

Many insurance companies offer add-on coverages to existing coverages in addition to – or instead of – policies that specifically address cybersecurity. Standalone policies that focus on cybersecurity typically provide more comprehensive coverage than a combination of add-ons. Again, companies will need to consider their needs, risks, and budgetary restrictions when deciding between these two approaches to coverage.

Ninety percent of data breaches are the result of human error instead of a malicious third party.[40] Companies should ensure that these accidental breaches are covered by their cybersecurity policy prior to purchase. Social engineering coverage may cover user error resulting from a psychological manipulation attack.

Some cybersecurity incidents are the result of an APT (Advanced Persistent Threat). APTs are a series of actions, events, and plans lasting weeks, months, or years. Many types of cybersecurity insurance coverage have time limits, which could lead to problems when a forensic team identifies events and damages that occur outside of the covered time range. Companies should see how the cyber insurance policy handles APTs, or if APTs are covered at all.

Cyber-attackers often target third-party vendors of larger companies, intending to use their illegal access of the third-party vendor's IT resources to attack the larger company's data or IT assets. Companies should review the potential cybersecurity insurance products to determine if these types of indirect attacks are covered.

Notes

1 Edward Gately, Cyber Insurance Market to Jump in 2021 as Cybercrime Surges, https://www.channelpartnersonline.com/2020/12/24/cyber-insurance-market-to-jump-in-2021-as-cybercrime-surges/ (last visited Mar 2, 2021).
2 Cowbell Cyber, Survey Results: The Economic Impact of Cyber Insurance (Small and Mid-Size Enterprises in the U.S.).
3 Bethan Moorcraft, US Cyber Insurance Market at Exciting Crossroad (2020), https://www.insurancebusinessmag.com/us/news/cyber/us-cyber-insurance-market-at-exciting-crossroad-236496.aspx (last visited Mar 2, 2021).
4 Mike Elgan, Cybersecurity Insurance Pros and Cons: Is it the Best Policy? https://securityintelligence.com/articles/cybersecurity-insurance-pros-and-cons/ (last visited Mar 3, 2021)
5 Wendi Whitmore, Why Cities Shouldn't Pay Ransomware Criminals, https://securityintelligence.com/posts/why-cities-shouldnt-pay-ransomware-criminals/ (last visited Mar 3, 2021).
6 Eric Chabrow, 10 Concerns When Buying Cyber Insurance, https://www.bankinfosecurity.com/10-concerns-when-buying-cyber-insurance-a-4859 (last visited Mar 3, 2021).
7 Tom Johansmeyer, Cybersecurity Insurance Has a Big Problem, https://hbr.org/2021/01/cybersecurity-insurance-has-a-big-problem (last visited Mar 3, 2021).
8 Raytheon Company, 2015 Industry Drill-Down Report: Financial Services, https://www.websense.com/assets/reports/report-2015-industry-drill-down-finance-en.pdf (last visited Mar 3, 2021).
9 Cynthia Harvey, Top 10 Cyber Insurance Companies in 2021, https://www.esecurityplanet.com/products/cyber-insurance-companies/ (last visited Mar 2, 2021).

10 Zack Whittaker, Cyber Insurer Chubb Had Data Stolen in Maze Ransomware Attack, https://techcrunch.com/2020/03/26/chubb-insurance-breach-ransomware/ (last visited Mar 3, 2021).

11 Andrew G. Simpson, Federal Judge Sides with Chubb in Denial of Target's Data Breach Bank Claims, https://www.insurancejournal.com/news/national/2021/02/10/600678.htm (last visited Mar 3, 2021).

12 Cynthia Harvey, Top 10 Cyber Insurance Companies in 2021, https://www.esecurityplanet.com/products/cyber-insurance-companies/ (last visited Mar 2, 2021).

13 Nicole Lindsey, AIG Case Highlights Complexities of Covering Cyber-Related Losses, https://www.cpomagazine.com/cyber-security/aig-case-highlights-complexities-of-covering-cyber-related-losses/ (last visited Mar 3, 2021).

14 Jeff Stone, AIG Must Cover Client's $5.9 Million in Cyber-Related Losses, Judge Rules, https://www.cyberscoop.com/aig-cyber-insurance-ssc-technologies/ (last visited Mar 3, 2021).

15 Cynthia Harvey, Top 10 Cyber Insurance Companies in 2021, https://www.esecurityplanet.com/products/cyber-insurance-companies/ (last visited Mar 2, 2021).

16 Cynthia Harvey, Top 10 Cyber Insurance Companies in 2021, https://www.esecurityplanet.com/products/cyber-insurance-companies/ (last visited Mar 2, 2021).

17 Cynthia Harvey, Top 10 Cyber Insurance Companies in 2021, https://www.esecurityplanet.com/products/cyber-insurance-companies/ (last visited Mar 2, 2021).

18 Cynthia Harvey, Top 10 Cyber Insurance Companies in 2021, https://www.esecurityplanet.com/products/cyber-insurance-companies/ (last visited Mar 2, 2021).

19 Cynthia Harvey, Top 10 Cyber Insurance Companies in 2021, https://www.esecurityplanet.com/products/cyber-insurance-companies/ (last visited Mar 2, 2021).

20 Cynthia Harvey, Top 10 Cyber Insurance Companies in 2021, https://www.esecurityplanet.com/products/cyber-insurance-companies/ (last visited Mar 2, 2021).

21 Andrew G. Simpson, AmTrust, Ex-CFO to Pay $10.5M to Settle SEC Charges of Improper Reporting, https://www.insurancejournal.com/news/national/2020/06/18/572740.htm (last visited Mar 4, 2021).

22 Dan Burke, Cyber 101: Understand the Basics of Cyber Liability Insurance, https://woodruffsawyer.com/cyber-liability/cyber-101-liability-insurance-2021/ (last visited Mar 2, 2021).

23 Iconic IT, Employee Cyber security Awareness Training: Are Employees Your Biggest Threat?, https://iconicit.com/cyber security/cyber security-awareness-training/ (last visit Mar 2, 2021).

24 Dan Burke, Cyber 101: Understand the Basics of Cyber Liability Insurance, https://woodruffsawyer.com/cyber-liability/cyber-101-liability-insurance-2021/ (last visited Mar 2, 2021).

25 Marianne Bonner, What Does a Cyber Liability Policy Cover?, https://www.thebalancesmb.com/what-s-covered-under-a-cyber-liability-policy-462459 (last visited Mar 2, 2021).

26 Marianne Bonner, What Does a Cyber Liability Policy Cover?, https://www.thebalancesmb.com/what-s-covered-under-a-cyber-liability-policy-462459 (last visited Mar 2, 2021).

27 Dan Burke, Cyber 101: Understand the Basics of Cyber Liability Insurance, https://woodruffsawyer.com/cyber-liability/cyber-101-liability-insurance-2021/ (last visited Mar 2, 2021).

28 Dan Burke, Cyber 101: Understand the Basics of Cyber Liability Insurance, https://woodruffsawyer.com/cyber-liability/cyber-101-liability-insurance-2021/ (last visited Mar 2, 2021).

29 Dan Burke, Cyber 101: Understand the Basics of Cyber Liability Insurance, https://woodruffsawyer.com/cyber-liability/cyber-101-liability-insurance-2021/ (last visited Mar 2, 2021).

30 Iconic IT, Cyber Risk Insurance: Choosing the Best Policy for Your Small to Medium-Sized Business, https://iconicit.com/blog/cyber-risk-insurance-choosing-the-best-policy-for-your-small-to-medium-sized-business/ (last visited Mar 2, 2021).

31 Iconic IT, Cyber Risk Insurance: Choosing the Best Policy for Your Small to Medium-Sized Business, https://iconicit.com/blog/cyber-risk-insurance-choosing-the-best-policy-for-your-small-to-medium-sized-business/ (last visited Mar 2, 2021).

32 FM Global, Cyber Insurance May Create False Sense of Security Among Senior Financial Executives at World's Top Companies, Suggests FM Global Survey, https://newsroom.fmglobal.com/releases/cyber-insurance-may-create-false-sense-of-security-among-senior-financial-executives-at-worlds-top-companies-suggests-fm-global-survey (last visited Mar 4, 2021).

33 Jeff Holmes, As Cyber Risks Grow, So Does the Need for Small Business Coverage, https://www.insurancejournal.com/magazines/mag-features/2020/04/20/565224.htm (last visited Mar 2, 2021)

34 Thomas-Fenner-Woods Agency Incorporated, How Much Cyber Liability Insurance Should A Business Purchase, https://www.tfwinsurance.com/2018/03/06/how-much-cyber-liability-insurance-should-a-business-purchase/ (last visited Mar 2, 2021).

35 BusinessWire, Bank of America Merchant Services' Third Annual Small Business Payments Spotlight Offers Small Business Owners Tips to Gain Customer Loyalty and a Competitive Edge, https://www.businesswire.com/news/home/20190909005294/en/Bank-of-America-Merchant-Services%E2%80%99-Third-Annual-Small-Business-Payments-Spotlight-Offers-Small-Business-Owners-Tips-to-Gain-Customer-Loyalty-and-a-Competitive-Edge (last visited Mar 4, 2021).

36 Jeff Holmes, As Cyber Risks Grow, So Does the Need for Small Business Coverage, https://www.insurancejournal.com/magazines/mag-features/2020/04/20/565224.htm (last visited Mar 2, 2021).

37 Connecting Point, Why Your Small-to-Medium Sized Business Should Consider Cyber Liability Insurance, https://www.cpcolorado.com/2020/06/why-your-small-to-medium-sized-business-should-consider-cyber-liability-insurance/ (last visited Mar 2, 2021).

38 Connecting Point, Why Your Small-to-Medium Sized Business Should Consider Cyber Liability Insurance, https://www.cpcolorado.com/2020/06/why-your-small-to-medium-sized-business-should-consider-cyber-liability-insurance/ (last visited Mar 2, 2021).

39 Connecting Point, Why Your Small-to-Medium Sized Business Should Consider Cyber Liability Insurance, https://www.cpcolorado.com/2020/06/why-your-small-to-medium-sized-business-should-consider-cyber-liability-insurance/ (last visited Mar 2, 2021).

40 Anthony Spadafora, 90 Percent of Data Breaches Are Caused by Human Error, https://www.techradar.com/news/90-percent-of-data-breaches-are-caused-by-human-error (last visited Mar 2, 2021).

4

The Compliance Laws of the GDPR, CCPA, and CMMC

GDPR

As a wave of data privacy rights, discussions, laws, and actions has swept over the world recently, especially so since World War II, one can suggest that for GDPR, or the General Data Protection Regulation, the Holocaust has had everything to do with its inception and passage.[1]

Enacted in May of 2018, the GDPR is designed to protect the data of its member states' owners, both in terms of cyber breach protection as well as data owners' rights to see their data, be forgotten, and/or see to the removal of that data.

Like the HIPAA legislation in the US, GDPR expands to cover EU citizen data surrounding almost all personal elements, including not only the obvious such as name, address, birth date, phone and credit card numbers, etc. but also religious affiliation, sexual orientation, political opinions, race, gender, and more.

History refresher: Concern of privacy data is directly linked to the atrocities of the Nazis who, as their regime rose to power, systematically abused private data to identify Jews and other minority groups with extreme objectives – the most atrocious of course being genocide, torture, manipulation, and other terrible acts.

Here are some facts surrounding early data processing during World War II that you will find curious if not disturbing:

In 1930s Germany, census workers went door to door filling out punch cards that indicated residents' nationalities, native language, religion and profession. The cards were counted by the early data processors known as Hollerith machines, manufactured by IBM's German subsidiary at the time, Deutsche Hollerith Maschinen GmbH (Dehomag). This history became more widely known after the publication of the 2001 book IBM

DOI: 10.1201/9781003023685-4

and the Holocaust: The Strategic Alliance Between Nazi Germany and America's Most Powerful Corporation, which argued that those Hollerith machines not only identified Jews, but also ran the trains that transported them to concentration camps. Some historians dispute the book's claims that IBM supported the use of its machines to carry out genocide and argue that the Nazis also used other methods, as simple as pen and paper, to round up victims just as effectively; the company hasn't denied that its machines were used during the Holocaust, but claims "most" documents about the operations have been "lost."[2]

Clearly this example indicates moral and ethical responsibility to ensure that as technology progresses, so too do the protections and rights involving personal data.

Implications for Business and Cybersecurity

Simply stated, businesses that fail to implement proper cyber protections into their data processing and infrastructure, in addition to the user/owner data rights and policies, can find themselves in breach of the Regulation.

In fact, negligence leading to data breach, data misuse, or failure to disclose or grant the rights enumerated under GDPR can lead to some *whopping* fines.

Specifically, Article 82, the Right to compensation and liability states:

> 5. Infringements of the following provisions shall, in accordance with paragraph 2, be subject to administrative fines up to 20 000 000 EUR, or in the case of an undertaking, up to 4 % of the total worldwide annual turnover of the preceding financial year, whichever is higher

Yeah, you're reading that correctly – 4% of global revenue or 20 million EUR, <u>whichever is higher.</u>

Think of the implications of this for companies such as Facebook, for example. Rounding out their 2019 revenue to $70 billion, that's 2.8 billion in fines. Ouch! A small company providing a data service provider role (say a growing SaaS company) of only a million in revenue could face a fine (the "higher of the two") of much more than just a $40,000 fine. Although wise judicial arbiters will make the fine appropriate to the offense, they still have the power to levy much more than the 4% for smaller companies.

"So why should I care?" you may be saying, "I don't do business in the US!" But what if you are a technology company and you have garnered European clients over the years. Many technology businesses have, or businesses such as the hotel industry, where technology is used to store the data of its European clients.

While it may be true that European regulators may not have power in the US, they could block your company from doing business in the EU, and that could sting.

One other scenario and implication is that your business may not service EU citizens directly, but your systems and services may service those companies who do, such as SaaS platforms or POS systems for hotels and other industries. Faults and flaws or failure to patch, keep up with vulnerabilities in your software could cause your company liability should it be determined your clients suffered privacy data loss or inability to otherwise comply with the Regulation. That now resonates with many businesses in the US.

More about GDPR

Running a cybersecurity company, I tend to think about GDPR from a cyber protection and risk management perspective. However, the implications for legal issues such as consent, declaration, and rights-granting policies and technologies also come into play.

Here are the seven key principles GDPR sets out to achieve:

- Lawfulness, fairness and transparency.
- Purpose limitation.
- Data minimization.
- Accuracy.
- Storage limitation.
- Integrity and confidentiality (security)
- Accountability.

To summarize, GDPR states that personal data must be "processed" lawfully, fairly, and in a transparent manner in relation to the data "subject." This means that all data controllers must only process data for the purpose they acquired it and with consideration of the data subject's rights. Finally, processed data must be stored, processed, and transmitted securely and with information security policy which will mitigate the risk of data breach or data theft.

DPO, DCs, and DPs

With GDPR, organizations now have the requirement to categorize themselves as Data Controllers and/or Data Processors. They also have the requirement to designate a Data Privacy Officer or DPO.

A Data Controller is a person, company, or other body that determines the purpose and means of personal data processing (this can be determined alone, or jointly with another person/company/body). For the official GDPR definition of "data controller," please see Article 4.7 of the GDPR.

The Data Controller determines the purposes for which and the means by which personal data is processed. The Data Processor processes personal data only on behalf of the controller. The data processor is usually a third party external to the company (credit card processors, for example)

Here is the official definition by the ICO or International Commissioner's office, the governing body in the UK for GDPR.

> "controller" means the natural or legal person, public authority, agency or other body which, alone or jointly with others, determines the purposes and means of the processing of personal data.
>
> "processor" means a natural or legal person, public authority, agency or other body which processes personal data on behalf of the controller.[3]

The relevance here is that controllers basically own and are liable for the data they're processing and for what purposes.

"Processors act on behalf of the relevant controller and under their authority. In doing so, they serve the controller's interests rather than their own."

Although a processor may make its own day-to-day operational decisions, Article 29 says it should only process personal data in line with a controller's instructions, unless it is required to do otherwise by law.

If a processor acts without the controller's instructions in such a way that it determines the purpose and means of processing, including to comply with a statutory obligation, it will be a controller in respect of that processing and will have the same liability as a controller.

A processor can be a company or other legal entity (such as an incorporated partnership, incorporated association, or public authority), or an individual, for example a consultant.[4]"

Governing these policies and processes in the organization is the DPO or The Data Protection Officer. The DPO

> ensures, in an independent manner, that an organization applies the laws protecting individuals' personal data. The designation, position and tasks of a DPO within an organization are described in Articles 37, 38 and 39 of the European Union General Data Protection Regulation.[5]

In short, it is the DPO's responsibility to ensure compliance with the GDPR. Since most organizations won't have a DPO, this resource can be outsourced.

Conclusions on GDPR

At the time of this writing, 2.5 years out, what has been the impact of GDPR? It is perhaps too early to tell, but just observe the changes:

- Most websites that track you are now telling you and allowing you to accept or not.
- GDPR has created a one-stop shop system for the regulation and enforcement of privacy in the EU.
- Other regulations, particularly in the United States (and we'll discuss CCPA next) have incorporated many of GDPR's principles and the result has influenced legislation.
- Corporate officers now have data privacy and protection as a discussion where a decade ago less so.

California Consumer Privacy Act (CCPA)

Introduced on January 3rd, 2018, and signed into law by then Governor Jerry Brown, the California Consumer Privacy Act or CCPA is what I consider the little brother of GDPR. It is a California-specific statute intended to "enhance privacy rights and consumer protection for residents.[6]"

Some of the differences, besides the obvious being the protection of only California residents:

- The GDPR language protects data *subjects*, defined as "an identified or identifiable natural person," whereas the CCPA gives certain rights to *consumers*, defined as "a natural person who is a California resident." ... The GDPR protects data subjects, not citizens or residents, unlike the CCPA.
- GDPR affects any organization inside or outside of the EU that offers goods or services to or monitors the behavior of EU subjects whereas CCPA is more limited:
  - Only companies or entities that do business with California residents and have a gross revenue of greater than $25 million, and handle personal data of more than 50,000 consumers for commercial purposes, or derive 50% or more of its annual revenues from selling consumers' personal data.

Other key facts about CCPA include[7]:

- No DPO or privacy officer designation is required as with GDPR.
- **Fines:** Civil penalties, which are violations lacking intent, are $2,500 per violation. *Intentional* violations are $7,500 each after notice and a 30-day opportunity to remedy the violations.
- **Security:** Does not define or impose data security requirements, but it does give consumers the right to take legal action and establishes a right of action if a security breach occurs. Note – this is the big kicker with CCPA. In a litigious society, CA residents have another way to be even more litigious!

Consent, rights of opting out of the sale of personal data, and legal right to take action are the foundation of CCPA. Many other minor differences between GDPR and CCPA exist but for purposes of this brief chapter I've highlighted what I think are the main ones.

The message here to corporate officers everywhere is simple: Protect your data, provide appropriate consent and methods of appropriate data removal or "unsubscription," and secure privacy data at rest, in transmission, and wherever processed to protect against consequential data breach and leakage!

Cybersecurity Maturity Model Certification (CMMC)

In this segment, I want to thank the amazing Webcheck Security practitioner Lori Crooks for her vast DoD, NIST, and other experience in sharing much of the following knowledge regarding CMMC! Built upon best security practices, the CMMC was organized by the Office of the Under Secretary of Defense for Acquisition and Sustainment (OUSD(A&S)) in recognition that *security is foundational to acquisition* and *should not be traded along with cost, schedule, and performance moving forward.*

Hence, CMMC was designed to protect all Department of Defense (DoD) contractors and *all related subcontractors.* CMMC was designed leveraging existing standards such as NIST 800-171, Aerospace Industries Association (AIA) National Aerospace Standard (NAS) 9933 "Critical Security Controls for Effective Capability in Cyber Defense," and Computer Emergency Response Team (CERT) Resilience Management Model (RMM) v1.2.

It primarily applies to Controlled Unclassified Information or information that the Government creates or possesses, or that an *entity* creates or possess for or on behalf of the Government that a law, regulation, or Government-wide policy requires or permits an agency to handle using safeguarding or dissemination controls. This could include defense information, financial information, privacy information, law enforcement, proprietary business information, etc.

Version 1.0 was released in January 2020 and later that year the requirements were solidified and training/certification infrastructure established. 2021 saw the implementation of the CMMC.

CMMC will have a profound impact in the next two years and beyond, on many manufacturers, information and data processors or service providers, SaaS companies, and technical providers. This is because the supply chain servicing DoD and other government entities is vast and broad.

Let's say for example that I have a contract with the Air Force to manufacture a particular widget that goes into the F-35. As part of that widget or assembly, I get certain pre-fabbed parts or other widgets, data or other services from Company B. Because Company B is part of that supply chain, and because I have been asked by the Air Force to certify as CMMC compliant, I must also ask Company B to certify.

CMMC certification for vendors/suppliers is likely to cost between $15k on the low end to $50k in *preparation* and $20k to $50k just to certify. Factors affecting this include:

- The scope and breadth of services and locations including how much CUI you handle – store, process, transmit, etc.
- IT infrastructure involved in your "widgets" or services
- Timeframes, i.e. can you phase this in over a year or do you need a time/resource investment *now* with a 3–6 month deadline?
- Consultant and assessor costs
- The required Maturity Level of the contract(s) you are maintaining or pursuing

Conceivably, a larger company with many contracts, some of which will require Level 5 Maturity, could spend upwards of $100k going through the certification process. Presumably, however, the said company would already have many of the NIST 800-171 or other controls largely in place.

Who Cares?

This leads to a simple answer to a simple question: To whom does CMMC apply? The answer is it will be specified in your RFI, RFP, or contract with the government or the contractors to whom you supply labor, parts, or services.

So, if you want to continue supplying, or compete to supply, certain federal government agencies and/or their subcontractors (i.e. your clients) then this affects you.

Levels

CMMC is broken into five Maturity tiers. Based on the already-established NIST 800-171, it has 110 controls and those controls are split across CMMC Levels 1–3. That means all 110 controls are encompassed within the Level 3 Practices, and at the Level 3 Maturity requirement, a certification by a 3PAO signifying Third Party Assessment Organization, will be required. 173 practices in total are mapped across the five Maturity Levels.

The simple overview of the CMMC Maturity Level lists the Level, the Processes, and the Practices:

1. **Level 1:** Performed. Basic Cyber Hygiene
2. **Level 2:** Documented. Intermediate Cyber Hygiene
3. **Level 3:** Managed. Good Cyber Hygiene
4. **Level 4:** Reviewed. Proactive
5. **Level 5:** Optimizing. Advanced/Progressive

Summary

3PAOs are governed by the CMMC Accreditation Board (AB), and certify all assessors. The bottom line here with CMMC is that if you are providing widgets or services to any entity that supplies the federal government (or if you supply the federal government directly), chances are this framework will touch you in at least a Level 1 or 2 Maturity Level. If you are required in your contracts to have a Level 3 Maturity or above, you will have to hire a 3PAO to help you certify or at least a risk and compliance consulting organization such as Webcheck Security to help you prepare or bring your practices and policies into alignment.[8]

Notes

1 See article BY OLIVIA B. WAXMAN, MAY 24, 2018 7:12 PM EDT, https://time.com/5290043/nazi-history-eu-data-privacy-gdpr/.
2 IBID.
3 ICO   https://ico.org.uk/for-organisations/guide-to-data-protection/ guide-to-the-general-data-protection-regulation-gdpr/controllers-and-processors/what-are-controllers-and-processors/.
4 https://ico.org.uk/for-organisations/guide-to-data-protection/guide-to-the-general-data-protection-regulation-gdpr/controllers-and-processors/what-are-controllers-and-processors/#4.
5 https://en.wikipedia.org/wiki/Data_Protection_Officer.
6 For more information see https://en.wikipedia.org/wiki/California_Consumer_Privacy_Act.

7 Comparing CCPA and GDPR: 8 Key Differences Between the Privacy Lawshttps://www.osano.com/articles/gdpr-vs-ccpa.

8 Further source information regarding CMMC can be found here: https://www.acq.osd.mil/cmmc/index.html.

5
CONCLUSIONS

This book has covered the topics of Cyber Risk, the Controls that are associated with them, Cybersecurity Insurance Policies, and the various Compliance Laws (most notably those of the GDPR, CCPA, and the CMMC) that help to enforce their statutes and provisions to make sure that the implemented Controls are working effectively in protecting the confidential information and data (most notably that of the Personal Identifiable Information (PII) datasets of both customers and employees).

In this chapter, we not only summarize what each chapter has covered, but also cover other important areas.

Chapter 1

In Chapter 1, the following concepts were covered:

- What Cyber Measurement Is All About;
- The Concept of Bayesian Measurement;
- The Statistical Methods of Measurement;
- The Various Quantitative Methods for Gauging Cyber Risk;
- The Decomposition of the One for One Substitution Cyber Risk Model;
- How to Reduce the Level of Cyber Risk with Bayesian Techniques;
- How to Reduce the Level of Cyber Risk with More Sophisticated Bayesian Techniques;
- The Beta Distribution;
- A Brief Overview into Cybersecurity Metrics.

While this chapter does get into the details of what Cyber Risk is all about, it is important to note that how it is specifically calculated, both from a mathematical and a statistical standpoint will vary greatly upon the security requirements of the company in question. But no matter how Cyber Risk is defined and computed, it is important for all departments and/or divisions in particular to have the ability to share that risk. No one entity should shoulder this entire responsibility.

Here are some ways in which it can be shared:

1) <u>You Need to Convey What the True Costs of Cyber Risk Are</u>
At present, the average cost for combating a Cyberattack is well above $1.1 million, and there is only a 37% chance that your company will be able to fully regain their brand reputation in case it is has been impacted. With such high statistics, the odds are that you may even have to close down operations, which will of course result in job loss. These numbers need to be disclosed to employees in all your departments so that they can come to grips with it as well as understand the sheer importance of maintaining good levels of Cyber Hygiene to mitigate the risks of losing their employment.

2) <u>Distribute Responsibility Accordingly</u>
Employees are often considered to be the weakest link in the security chain. But they don't have to be. According to the latest Verizon Data Breach Investigations Report, 93% of all Cyber-related breaches come down to phishing-related attacks. Had the employees of these organizations been given proper training, the probability of being hit in this aspect would be much lower. The subconscious view of this is that ok, so what if we are hit? Our Cyber specialists can fix it, right? Well, the answer to this is plainly wrong. The IT Security teams are so overburdened these days that they may not be able to respond quickly to cut down any further risk that has been posed by this scenario, thus increasing the chances that the Cyberattacker can cause even more damage. In the training that they are being given, you need to firmly emphasize to your employees that it is squarely their responsibility to keep an eye out for phishing emails and to respond to it appropriately by either deleting it or notifying the IT Security staff promptly. But of course, you need to give your employees the tools to do this and keep them updated on the latest trends of

phishing variants so that they can do their part to cut down this kind of Cyber Risk.

3) Share Information and Data with All Parties

Even today, there tend to be lines of divisions between the IT Department and the IT Security team. For example, with the former, they think that their job is to primarily make sure that the IT and Network Infrastructure is running at optimal levels, and the latter thinks that all they need to do is simply stay ahead of the Cyber threat curve. While these are their unique job functions, the truth of the matter is that the two go hand in hand with another in order to keep your company well protected. Thus, any information/data about the Cyber Threat Landscape should not just be kept in individual silos. It needs to be shared, to varying degrees, with all departments of your company that should have access to it. For example, research has shown that it takes at least 60 minutes (and probably even more) for a CIO and/or CISO as well as their team to respond to a security breach. This is primarily due to the lack of the communications flows that have been deployed. This response time needs to be cut down to just a matter of minutes. But this of course can only be done if those silos of information/data are shared among one another.

4) Deploy the Right Cybersecurity Framework

One of the best ways in which you share the responsibility of Cyber Risk throughout your company is to implement a good Framework and the appropriate Controls that will support it. Some of the more commonly used ones are as follows:

- The PCI DSS;
- The ISO 27001/27002;
- The NIST Framework for Improving Critical Infrastructure Security.

While all of this is good, there is yet another good Framework that is now prominent. This is known as the "Zero Trust Framework". In other words, you cannot trust anything in your environment. Everything and anything should be assumed to be a risk. The motto here is: "Never Trust, Always Verify".

Chapter 3

In Chapter 2, the various Cyber Audit Frameworks and the specific Control Sets were examined in great detail. In summary, here is what was covered:

- An Overview into Cybersecurity Controls;
- A Technical Review into the Cybersecurity Audit;
- A Review of the Cyber Audit Frameworks;
- The Cyber Risk Controls.

It is important to keep in mind that conducting a Cyber Audit is essentially conducting a thorough and deep and dive-based Risk Assessment. Once all of the vulnerabilities, gaps, and weaknesses have been uncovered through this process, then the appropriate Cyber Controls can be put in place in order to mitigate those risks from precipitating into full-blown security breaches.

But in the end, no matter how much the lines of defenses of a particular business have been beefed up, every entity is prone to becoming a victim of a Cyberattack. The key here is in being proactive and having the ability to bounce back and restore mission critical operations in just a matter of a few hours, or even less, if possible. This is where the concept of "Cyber Resiliency" comes into play.

A technical definition of Cyber Resiliency is as follows:

Cyber resilience is the ability to prepare for, respond to and recover from cyber-attacks. It helps an organization protect against cyber risks, defend against, and limit the severity of attacks, and ensure its continued survival despite an attack. Cyber resilience has emerged over the past few years because traditional cyber security measures are no longer enough to protect organizations from the spate of persistent attacks.[1]

An Example of Cyber Resiliency

Let us illustrate this definition with an example. Suppose that Company XYZ has invested in all of the latest security technologies imaginable; despite taking all of these safeguards, they are still hit with a large scale Cyberattack, such as that of ransomware.

Not many companies can withstand such an attack, and in most cases, they would most likely decide to go ahead and pay the money that is demanded of them so that they can resume mission critical operations ASAP.

But company ZYX decided not to go this route. They refused to pay the hacking group in question, because they realized that if they did pay up, there is no guarantee that they will not be impacted again by the same Cyberattacker, and asking for more money the second time around. In this regard, company XYZ played their cards right because they maintained a very proactive mindset.

With this, they created backups on a daily basis, and they also made use of a Cloud-based Infrastructure in which to host their entire IT and Network Infrastructure. Because of this, they were able to basically kill any of the virtual machines and the virtual desktops that were impacted by the ransomware, and within just a few hours, they were able to build new ones again and transfer all information and data to them from the backups.

So, within a day or so, company XYZ was back up on their feet running again, as if nothing had ever occurred. As it is legally required, the CISO of this company contacted all of the necessary law enforcement officials, notified key stakeholders of what had happened (especially their customers), and immediately launched a forensic investigation to determine what had exactly happened. The next mandate was to update all of the relevant Security Policies in order to reflect on the lessons that have been learned from this incident.

How the Definition of Cyber Resiliency Was Met

So as our illustration points out, company XYZ met all of the components of Cyber resiliency because they were able to:

- Greatly limit the impacts of the ransomware attack;
- They were able to ensure its survival in just a matter of a day or two;
- They are now prepared to mitigate the risk of the same threat vector (or for that matter, any of its variants) from happening again.

So, Cyber resiliency simply does not refer to how a business can just operate at *baseline levels* after being impacted. Rather, it refers to the fact as to how a business can resume operations back up to a *100% normal speed* in the shortest time that is possible and reduce the chances of becoming a victim again.

What Is the Difference between Cyber Resiliency and Cybersecurity?

There is often a great deal of confusion between the two, so here are the key differences:

Cybersecurity refers to the tools that are used to protect both digital and physical assets. So in the case of Company XYZ, this would include the routers, firewalls, network intrusion devices, proximity readers, key FOBS, etc. to protect the Intellectual Property (IP), the databases which contain the PII of both employees and customers, shared resources that are stored on the corporate servers, access to the secure rooms which contain actual client files, etc.

Cyber resiliency refers to how well company XYZ can fully get into the mindset of a Cyberattacker to anticipate the new tools as well as their elements of surprise for preventing them from penetrating into the company's lines of defenses and causing long-lasting damage.

In other words, Cybersecurity deals with the prevention of theft of information and data at just one point in time. Cyber resiliency is designed to protect the business from being permanently knocked off the grid multiple times. The former takes a pure technological approach, while the latter takes a much more psychological approach, which encompasses all facets of human behavior and the culture at Company XYZ.

The NIST Special Publication 800-160 Volume 2

This bulletin (aka "Cyber Resiliency Considerations for the Engineering of Trustworthy Secure Systems") details the specific Controls that a business must implement in order to come to an acceptable level of Cyber resiliency. This is provided in Table 5.1.

Apart from having the ability to properly calculate Cyber Risk, having the appropriate set of Cyber Controls to mitigate those

Table 5.1 The Goals Of the NIST SP 800-160 Controls

THE CONTROL	IT'S PRIMARY OBJECTIVE
Adaptive Response	Have the ability and means to respond to a security breach in a quick and efficient manner
Analytic Monitoring	Be able to detect any anomalous or abnormal behavioral patterns quickly
Coordinated Projection	The need to implement multiple layers of authentication
Deception	Purposely confuse the Cyberattacker with regard to the main points of entry
Diversity	Use different kinds of techniques to further minimize the level of risk
Dynamic Positioning	Increase rapid recovery by further diversifying the main nodes of network communications distribution
Dynamic Representation	The importance of understanding the interlinkages between Cyber and non-Cyber resources
Non-Persistence	Keep resources only on an as-needed basis
Privilege Restriction	Assign only the appropriate permissions, rights, and accesses to employees to conduct their daily job functions
Realignment	Keep changing the interlinks so that a breakdown in non-critical assets will not have a cascading effect on the critical assets
Redundancy	Implement multiple instances of critical assets
Segmentation	Separate the Network Infrastructure into different subnets
Substantiated Integrity	Determine if critical assets have been further corrupted
Unpredictability	Keep mixing up your lines of defenses so that the Cyberattacker cannot plan their course of action

particular levels of Cyber Risk, it is also very important for a business entity to carry out what is known as "Cybersecurity Insurance." This was the point of topic of Chapter 3, and it covered the following items:

- Cybersecurity Risk Insurance Policies;
- The State of the Cybersecurity Insurance Market;
- An Analysis of the Major Insurance Carriers That Offer Cyber Insurance;
- The Major Components of a Cyber Insurance Policy;
- How Should an SMB Decide on What Kind of Cyber Policy to Get.

But, there are other aspects as well to a Cyber Risk Insurance Policy, and all of the entities that are involved with it, ranging from the Insurance Carriers, to the Underwriters, and to the Policy Holders that need them. Some of these other areas include the following.

What Cybersecurity Insurance Is and Its History

In its broadest sense, Cybersecurity Insurance can be defined as follows:

> A cyber insurance policy, also referred to as cyber risk insurance or cyber liability insurance coverage (CLIC), is designed to help an organization mitigate risk exposure by offsetting costs involved with recovery after a cyber-related security breach or similar event.[2]

Cybersecurity Insurance is not a new product by any means. It actually has its roots going back to the late 1970s, when the Errors and Omissions concepts were first introduced. The first versions of Cybersecurity Insurance came out in the 1980s, which were primarily designed to help the losses covered by the large financial firms and other Fortune 500 companies.

But it was not until the late 1990s when interest in Cybersecurity Insurance policies started to grow in the marketplace. The primary catalyst for this growth were the fears of Y2K, which were cemented in the thoughts that there would be widespread computer shutdowns on a global basis. In this regard, it has been the Lloyd's of London which has been credited with offering the first true Cybersecurity Insurance policy.

This initiative was launched by Keith Daniels and Rob Hamesfahr, former attorneys at the law firm known as Blatt, Hamesfahr & Eaton. The underwriters for this first policy were Ian Hacker (who was an underwriter at Lloyd's of London), Ted Doolittle, and Kinsey Carpenter. The primary goal of this policy was to offer third party coverage for major business interruptions.

It should be noted that during this timeframe, there was no first party coverage offered. Also, these first types of Cybersecurity Insurance did not cover losses experienced by Insider Attacks caused by an employee with malicious intents, failure to come into compliance with any federal rules and regulations, and any fines or penalties that could be imposed onto a business entity by a regulatory body.

It was after the 9/11 attacks that interest in Cybersecurity Insurance spiked even further. This was because many leaders, both at the corporate and government levels, were starting to realize the gravity of

Cyberattacks. In this instance, the first types of threat vehicles were those of Trojan Horses, Viruses, and primitive forms of Malware.

Because of this, there was also the stark realization that it is not just physical attacks that can cause business interruptions, but that threats launched toward the virtual world could also bring an organization down to its knees. This type of loss was not covered by Cybersecurity Insurance during that timeframe. The primary for reason for this was that there was no historic data in which to calculate and measure and price this kind of risk. As a result, many insurance providers focused most of their offerings on those losses that were incurred by attacks to physical IT and Network Infrastructures.

But as Cyberattacks continued to mount and proliferate upon the Cloud (or Virtual) Infrastructures, the demand for Cybersecurity Insurance policies to cover this type of loss started to grow because of the sheer amount of Identity Theft and Data Breaches that were occurring.

Another catalyst that finally made the Insurance industry to cave in and to extend their policies to cover these kinds of losses was the passage of the "California Security Breach Information Act of 2003".

This law mandated that any entity that conducted business transactions in the State of California had to notify any customers if their PII was at risk because of a Cyberattack that occurred.

Many other States also passed and implemented similar laws rather quickly, and the European Union also passed similar laws with a major focus on the telecom providers and Internet Service Providers (ISPs).

Because of all of this, the major Insurance carriers now offered first party coverage to businesses and corporations (this includes such things as Forensics Investigations, Public Relations damage and repair, credit monitoring services offered to victims, and costs associated with notifying people that they may have been impacted).

Despite this, not all the Insurance carriers during this timeframe offered the same type of coverage to Corporate America. For example, many of the carriers had extremely strict sublimits still set in place and the amounts that were paid out differed greatly.

One of the reasons for this was that each carrier had varying risk tolerances that they were willing to take on and differing methodologies in quantifying what level of risk was acceptable or what was high. After all, Insurance providers are businesses themselves, and they want to make sure that they don't to take on too much of a burden if it is going to directly impact their bottom line.

The turning point that made the Insurance carriers loosen their strings was the horrific security breach that occurred at the retail giant known as TJ Maxx. In this attack, over 45 million credit card and debit card numbers were stolen, which cost the company almost $5 Billion. Over 25 class action lawsuits were filed, and the retailer had to dole out $177 Million in settlement claims. Even to this day, this Cyberattack has been deemed to be one of the worst in history.

To top this off, there were also those security breaches at Anthem Blue Cross Blue Shield and Target, in which over 10 Million credit card and debit card numbers were heisted. This only showed that despite the best lines of defenses that were being implemented, any business or corporation is at risk to a large scale Cyberattack. Thus, at present, the demand and need for a comprehensive Cybersecurity Insurance policy is at its highest point ever.

The Advantages and Disadvantages of Cybersecurity Insurance

This section of the book examines what a typical Cybersecurity Insurance policy covers (the advantages) and what it does not cover (the disadvantages).

The Advantages

Here is what is typically covered:

1) <u>Any Damage or Loss to Electronic Data</u>
   This includes any "damage, theft, disruption or corruption" to the Electronic Data that a business or corporation may possess. It even covers any loss or damage to your employee's workstations, laptops, or wireless devices. But in order to be provided coverage, there are two criteria that need to be met:
   • The Electronic Data that has been impacted must be the result of a Cyberattack;
   • Coverage will only be granted to the Electronic Data that resides on company-issued devices.
   This provision will also provide coverage to recover any hijacked, lost, or stolen Electronic Data, and even the costs

that are associated with hiring a specialist to accomplish this task.

2) Any Lost Income or Expenses Experienced by a Cyberattack

To a certain extent, many Insurance Providers will provide for any monetary loss as a result of a Cyberattack, whether it is lost revenue or extra expenses incurred because of it. However, this coverage is typically different than the normal coverage afforded by a standard Commercial Property Policy, which applies to only any monetary losses incurred to the physical property of a business entity.

3) Losses from Cyber Extortion

This can be specifically defined as follows:

Cyber extortion is the act of cyber-criminals demanding payment through the use of or threat of some form of malicious activity against a victim, such as data compromise or denial of service attack.[2]

Ransomware is a typical example of this. Under this kind of Cyberattack, the hacker sends out malware to your computer or server, which will lock up the screen and any other mission critical files that reside within it. The hacker will typically ask for a ransom, made payable by using a virtual currency, such as Bitcoin. Theoretically, once this is paid, the Cyberattacker should send you the decryption algorithm to decrypt and unlock your screen and files, but in reality, this hardly ever happens. Cybersecurity Insurance will cover this, from two perspectives:

- Any costs that are associated with responding to the Cyberattacker;
- Any ransom money that you have paid them.

4) Costs of Notification

After a security breach has impacted an organization, many regulations now require for the C-Suite to provide written notification to the affected stakeholders, which typically involve the customers, suppliers, etc. Cybersecurity Insurance will cover the following:

- The costs that are associated with notifying the stakeholders (such as letter preparation, the costs of sending the letters out, etc.);
- Any legal expenses;
- Providing credit monitoring services to the impacted stakeholders (this is typically for one year);
- In some cases, the costs that are associated with setting up a temporary call center in order to address stakeholder questions and concerns.

NOTE: These are known as "First Party Coverages" and are subject to a deductible based upon the type of Cybersecurity Insurance that you have.

It should be noted that Cybersecurity Insurance also provides for what are known as "Third Party Coverages", and these typically arise from claims that been filed by the impacted stakeholders against the organization and any type of monetary settlements that have been subsequently agreed upon. Typical examples of this include the following:

1) Network Security Liability

These kinds of claims arise when lawsuits are filed against a business entity when there has been a major breach, and the PII has been hijacked, as a result of a Distributed Denial of Service (DDoS) attack, Virus, Malware, or any unauthorized access to the database in which the PII resides in.

2) Network Privacy Liability

This is different from the network security liability, in which the Cybersecurity Insurance policy will cover any claims on the grounds that the organization did not adequately protect the PII that was stored on the database. Inadequate protection often refers to not deploying and applying the latest software patches and upgrades, letting unauthorized users gain access to the database when there was no need for them to in the first place, etc.

3) Electronic Media Liability

Typical examples of this include:

- Copyright Infringement;
- Domain Name Infringement.

Cybersecurity Insurance will only cover those instances if the listed items have been published and distributed maliciously over the Internet, without your prior knowledge.

The Disadvantages

Here is what is typically NOT covered:
1) Anything in Excess of Your Policy Limit or Sublimit
   Any costs or claims that have been filed that exceed your current Cybersecurity Insurance policy will not be covered. In these cases, if more coverage is needed, you will have to get a newer policy, which means it will be more expensive. A sublimit can be specifically defined as follows:

   A limitation in an insurance policy on the amount of coverage available to cover a specific type of loss. It places a maximum on the amount available to pay that type of loss, rather than providing additional coverage for that type of loss.[3]

   For example, a sublimit may be on the costs that are related to a Forensics Investigation, which would place a cap for that specific kind of activity.

2) Loss of Intellectual Property (IP) or Corporate Trade Secrets
   At present, Cybersecurity Insurance does not cover this because the industry cannot quantitatively gauge with certainty any losses that occur because of a devaluing in this area.
3) Loss to Reputation and Brand Damage
   The insurance industry has no current financial methodology to quantify the risk in these two areas. The present view is that it is up to the CIO or CISO to provide protections in this as well as for any financial expenses that are incurred.
4) Expenses Due to Business Interruptions or Downtime
   In this instance, any loss monetary loss incurred is not covered by a Cybersecurity Insurance policy.

5) <u>Any Security Breaches That Have Been Caused by Negligence</u>
The insurance industry will not provide coverage for an organization that maintains a level of poor "Cyber Hygiene". Although this is a qualitative term, this can stem from such things as not implementing a Security Policy, being out of compliance with regulatory agencies within the federal government, or even failure to maintain minimum standards that have been set forth by the insurance company that is providing the Cybersecurity Insurance.

6) <u>Threats Posed by Nation State Actors</u>
This can be specifically defined as follows:

They work for a government to disrupt or compromise target governments, organizations or individuals to gain access to valuable data or intelligence and can create incidents that have international significance.[4]

Insurance companies do not provide coverage for any hacks or Cyberattacks that have been ascertained as terrorist by nature. Typically, this will involve the Fortune 100 companies that have a large international dominance with a lot of PII at risk.

7) <u>Remediating IT Assets</u>
Any costs that are incurred to make an IT Asset more fortified after a Cyberattack is not covered.

8) <u>Losses to Physical Property</u>
As described earlier, Cybersecurity Insurance will typically cover only those losses that are deemed to be digital in nature. Thus, in this regard, any expenses incurred to the Physical Property of an organization will not be covered. So, for example, if there was a Cyberattack that damaged the Critical Infrastructure to a city (such as the water supply, electrical power grids, oil/gas pipelines, etc.) these would not be covered.

It is important to note at this point that the insurance industry is often criticized on two fronts:

- There are currently no efforts being undertaken to create quantitative financial models or developing other risk assessment tools so that more coverage, especially in the way of the intangible losses, can eventually be offered to businesses and corporations.
- Insurance companies are only providing Cybersecurity Insurance to make themselves more profitable. For example, according to a recent study by the Financial Times demonstrated that in 2017, the Loss Ratio (which is the monetary number of claims paid divided by the monetary amounts of premiums that have been paid in) was as high as 32%. For example, for every $1 Million in premiums that are being paid by an organization, only a mere $320,000 is being paid out in claims.[5]

The Factors That Insurance Companies Consider When Providing Coverage

When deciding upon when to award an applicant with a Cybersecurity Insurance policy, many insurance carriers take a close look as to what the organization is already doing in terms of fortifying their lines of defense.

These are all qualitative measures because as it has been pointed out throughout this book, there are currently no known financial models or other types of assessment tools in the insurance industry that can quantify the level of risk that an applicant possesses. At present, here is what a typical insurance company looks at before giving out a Cybersecurity Insurance policy:

1) If Perimeter Security Has Been Installed

   Typically, this includes a mixture of the use of Firewalls, Routers, and Network Intrusion devices. The insurance company wants to see that the organization has taken a proactive approach in deploying these tools to protect both their IT and Network Infrastructures.

2) Making Sure That There Is a Security Policy in Place and That It Is Being Enforced

   Although this is one of the first items that any business or corporation should address for their own sake, this is one of the key areas that gets looked at when an application is submitted for a Cybersecurity Insurance policy. An insurance company wants to see that it is being updated on a regular basis, and that *all employees* are abiding by the rules that have been set forth by it.

3) The Implementation of a Robust Password Policy

It is important to note that passwords are often the first target that the Cyberattacker will go after. After all, once he or she has this prized possession, they literally have the keys that can unlock the proverbial "crown jewels" of the unsuspecting victim. In fact, in many of the recent Cyberattacks, organizations have been blamed for enforcing poor Password Policies. Because of this, many insurance carriers are now scrutinizing business entities to make sure that have an airtight Password Policy in place. Typically, this is what they look for:

- Making sure that passwords are reset at regular intervals;
- Confirming that the passwords used are very difficult to crack;
- Employees are constantly trained in how to create a strong password.

In this instance, in order to meet the stringent requirements of the insurance industry, it is best if the organization has deployed the following:

- Multifactor Authentication: This is where another layer of security (such as the use of Biometric Technology), in addition to the password, is being used to fully authenticate the employee before they gain access to shared resources on the network drives;
- The use of a Password Manager: These are software applications that instantly create very long and complex passwords that are very difficult to break, and even resets the passwords used at regular intervals, without any intervention required by the employee.

4) Confirming That There Is a Regular Schedule for the Deployment of Software Patches and Upgrades

Even when the organization does this, there is still no guarantee that their servers, workstations, wireless devices, and other software applications won't be hit by a Cyberattack. But by doing this on a timely basis, it proves to the insurance carrier that the C-Suite is taking a very proactive stance in making sure that their systems are continually being updated.

5) Making Sure That the Network Lines of Communications between Remote Workers and the Corporate Headquarters Is Secure

This is another area that is a prime target for the Cyberattacker. If they can intercept any sort of communications in this fashion, then more than likely, he or she will be able to gain subsequent access through a backdoor in the IT or Network Infrastructure of an organization. As a result, insurance companies also take a close look as to what kinds of preventative measures have been taken so that this does not happen. Key areas that are looked at include the following:

- Has a Virtual Private Network (VPN) been installed?
- Is Two Factor Authentication (2FA) being used? For example, along with the password, is another security measure being used to authenticate the remote employee, such as an RSA Token?
- What are the standards of Encryption that are deployed?

6) The Types of Physical Access Controls That Have Been Installed

As it has been pointed out to earlier in this book, any security breaches caused to the physical premises of a business or a corporation are not covered by a Cybersecurity Insurance policy. But still, the levels of physical security that have been deployed by an organization are carefully looked at by the insurance carrier before a policy is awarded.

If the business entity meets or exceeds the above, then there is a good probability that it will be accepted as a policy holder by the insurance carrier. But it is also important to keep in mind that once this has occurred, the C-Suite needs to be proactive in maintaining their lines of defense, as an insurance company can conduct an in-depth audit at any point in time, they feel it is necessary.

Typically, this involves the following:

- Incident Response and Disaster Recovery plans are being practiced on a regular basis and the appropriate documentation is updated in real time when and as needed;
- Security Awareness Training, especially for employees, is being given on a regular basis as well;
- Any known and unknown gaps and vulnerabilities are being continually being remediated. This is typically done by conducting an exhaustive Penetration and/or Threat Hunting Test;
- Making sure that there are an adequate number of Controls in place in order to protect the PII and/or other types of regulated data that the organization has been entrusted with to store in their databases;
- Making sure that the business entity is up to speed in terms of compliance with both federal and state regulations;
- There are no repeated patterns of any security-related issues not being addressed and corrected.

By being proactive with the mentioned points, the C-Suite can more or less be guaranteed that they will receive the full amount of their claim after it has been filed. Finally, it is also equally important to keep in mind that simply because you have a Cybersecurity Insurance Policy, you will always be covered, no matter what. For example, everything that resides from within the IT and Network Infrastructures must be kept up to date and be assessed for any vulnerabilities, weaknesses, and gaps. Cybersecurity Insurance carriers are strict about this, and if you do not keep up to date, you could very well lose your policy in the end.

Chapter 4

Chapter 4 covered the Data Privacy Laws of both the GDPR and the CCPA. These Legislative Mandates have been created so that individuals now have much greater freedom when it comes to the control of how their personal information and data are being used by businesses and their external third parties. Businesses that originate in both the United States and the European Union must comply with them; if not, they can face some very harsh financial penalties, and even further, subsequent audits. But there is still confusion between the two of these, in that they are often viewed as being mirrors of each other.

However, this is far from the truth, and the following are some of the major differences between the GDPR and the CCPA.

PII Versus Personal Data

The CCPA has been designed to protect the *personal information* of American consumers, while the GDPR has been crafted to specially protect the *personal data* of individuals in the European Union (EU) and any other consumer that transacts commerce with a business with offices in the EU.

Personal information can be defined as follows:

- Legal full names, Email Addresses, Driver's Licenses, Social Security Cards, Passports, etc. In other words, anything that can identify a certain individual based upon a mixture of both letters and/or numbers.
- It is also extended to include:

  - The browsing history and current web-based activity of consumers;
  - Internet Cookies;
  - Any form of dynamic activity that takes place between a web form and mobile apps;
  - Social Media information, especially if it can be used to build a profile about an individual.

Personal data is defined as:

- Any specific piece of data that can *directly* identify a person. It is important to note that there has to be a direct correlation. This definition does not include any *inferences* between datasets that can be used to identify someone.

In this regard, the CCPA only has a foothold in regulating businesses that meet certain revenue qualifications. In contrast, the GDPR is much more heavily focused on regulating entities that are known as

Data Controllers, as these actually manage and process the personal information and data.

The Rights That Are Afforded to Individuals

While both the CCPA and the GDPR have established a common set of rights that are granted to consumers, there are also noticeable differences between the two of them as well, which are:

The CCPA

- Opting Out: Consumers located in California can request their PII data sets not be used, sold, or distributed in any fashion to external third parties.
- Non-Retaliation: If a consumer wishes to challenge a business as to how their personal information and data is being handled, they cannot treat that person differently than other customers. For example, that business must still allow the consumer their products and/or services, charge them at the same price as they would others, and provide the same quality of service to other customers who have not challenged them.
- The Use of Attorneys: Just like the right to having an attorney in a trial, a consumer has the right to hire a lawyer (or any other designated appointee) to represent them in the questioning, dispute, or contestation as to how their PII datasets are being stored, processed, and used.
- Any Use of Incentive Tactics: If any sort of financial motive were used in order to sell your PII dataset(s) to an external third party, that business in question must notify you immediately in writing.

The GDPR

- The Ability to Correct Mistakes: EU consumers have the right to ask the business to correct their personal information and data if it is found to be in error. In return, that entity must then make the changes immediately and provide proof of that in writing to the consumer.

- While the CCPA allows Californian consumers to prohibit the selling of their personal data, it is rather murky if it also allows them to stop the actual processing of it. In contrast, the GDPR directly spells out that EU consumers can restrict the actual processing of that data.
- The Profiling of Consumers: Any automated tool that is used (such as Artificial Intelligence and/or Machine Learning) to build and create a profile an individual is strictly prohibited.

The Usage of Data

There are also differences in how the personal data can be used.

The CCPA

This legislation allows for a much wider latitude for California-based businesses to use consumer information and data in a way that is legal. But they must provide written notification to customers as to how this is specifically being used. Once again, the right to opt out must be spelled out very clearly, especially contact forms that are used in both websites and mobile apps.

The GDPR

Unlike the CCPA, the GDPR very clearly spells out how the PII datasets can be used. There are six established rules for this, and at least one of them must be met before any kind of usage is deemed to be lawful:

- More Stringent Consent: EU citizens can opt out quite easily, but in order for their confidential information to be used, they must also give explicit approval to the business, in a manner known as "Opting In".
- The Contract: In order to use the data, a contract must be formed first between the business and the consumer, or at least be in the stages of formation.

- Controls: The right set of Controls must be implemented and carefully scrutinized first before any personal data can be distributed. Further, these Controls are subject to an audit by the appropriate regulatory agencies.
- Healthcare: Personal information/data can be used, no matter what, if it is used to save the life of an individual. This is directly applicable to Emergency Room situations.
- Public Usage: If the PII datasets of consumers are going to be used for the commonwealth of the public, then this must be directly stipulated to those groups of individuals that will be impacted in this regard.
- Mission Critical Operations: If the processing and usage of PII datasets are needed to support the most important processes of the business, then they can proceed, provided that written notification is provided to the consumers. This is deemed to be more of a murky area of the GDPR, and technically it is known as "Exploring Further".

Another piece of Legislation that has a close relationship to both the GDPR and the CCPA is what is known as the "CMMC". This is a mandate that protects the privacy of both the information and data that is shared in the Federal Government space and is dependent upon the Department of Defense (DoD) and the Defense Contractors and Subcontractors who award the bids and contracts. In summary, there are five distinct "Maturity Levels" that are associated with the CMMC, and at the present time, both Defense Contractors and their Subcontractors must have achieved certification at Maturity Level 1. This deals with the privacy and handling of the Federal Contract Information (FCI) datasets.

A technical definition of the FCI is as follows:

> Information, that is not intended for public release, that is provided by or generated for the Government under a contract to develop or deliver a product or service to the Government, but not including information provided by the Government to the public (such as on public websites) or simple transactional information, such as necessary to process payments.[1]

It is important to note that a CMMC Assessment for Maturity Level 1 is conducted and further evaluated in order to fully ensure that a contractor or even a subcontractor has come into compliance with the standards that have established and set forth by the CMMC. These assessments are conducted only by CMMC-based Third Party Assessment Organizations (C3PAOs) and Certified Assessors.

The Components of the Maturity Level 1

This section further examines these components and they are as follows.

The Access Control (AC) The biggest objective of this area is to strictly curtail the amount of access level that is given to authorized users or even the devices that are accessing the FCI datasets. Also, the definition of an authorized individual can be extended to those who are acting on behalf of them.

The goals here are to:

- Determine if all of the authorized individuals (who access the FCI datasets) are allowed to do so;
- Any and all processes that are accessing the FCI datasets can be ascertained;
- All devices that are accessing them can be properly identified;
- That the authorized users have only that level of access which they absolutely need;
- That only authorized processes are in place to query the FCI datasets;
- That only authorized devices are used to access this data.

This provision also includes the examination of Access Control Policies in the environment of the contractor or the subcontractor that can exist between active or passive individuals. Also, any mechanisms that are used to confirm the identity of individuals wishing to gain access to the FCI datasets must also be evaluated as well as associated user groups and profiles that contain the permission, rights and privileges.

Other provisions that can be further examined in this area include the following:

- The types of transactions and functions that are executed;
- Any external systems that are used to access the FCI datasets and the network connections that are established;
- Any public-related information that has been posted that can be inferentially traced back to the FCI datasets;
- The identification of all entities, agencies, devices, or processes that are acting on behalf of authorized contractors or subcontractors;
- Any and all individuals that could potentially have access to the FCI datasets and the mechanisms that are in place to authenticate them as well.

The Identification and Authentication (IA) This practice area deals with any agencies, users, entities, or processes that are acting on behalf of other authorized individuals or even devices, whether they are hard wired or wireless based.

The specific goals here are to:

- Confirm that all agencies, users, entities, or processes have been correctly identified.

This includes the following examples:

- MAC addresses;
- IP addresses;
- Unique token identifiers;
- Usernames/Passwords;
- Key Tokens;
- One-time passwords;
- Cryptographic devices.

Other provisions that can be further examined in this area include the following:

- Making sure that the required authentication mechanisms are in place to correctly identify all parties that are involved in accessing, processing, and storing of the FCI datasets.

The Media Protection (MP)   This practice area focuses upon either the clean wiping out of the physical media devices containing the FCI datasets that are no longer no needed. In technical terms, this simply means that any associated hardware that stores the information/data has been completely eradicated of it, and which also needs to be confirmed by a C3PAO or other third party CMMC Assessor.

This includes the following examples:

- Network-based devices;
- Scanners;
- Photocopy machines;
- Printers;
- Smartphones/tablets/notebooks;
- Paper;
- Microfilm.

It is important that the term "Sanitization" refers to the fact that the FCI datasets cannot be reconstructed or retrieved by any means whatsoever.

The Physical Protection (PE)   This practice area deals with the physical access of those environments, information systems, or any other devices that house any FCI datasets.

The specific goals here are to:

- Determine if only authorized individuals can gain physical access to the FCI datasets;
- The limitations that are in place to limit all types and kinds of physical access;
- The kinds of limiting mechanisms that are in place with respect to access to all sorts of equipment, whether they are hard wired or wireless;
- The kinds of limiting mechanisms that are in place with respect to access to the particular environments that house the physical media in which the FCI datasets reside.

Other statutes that can be further examined in this area include the following:

- External entities that are visiting or working at either contractor or the subcontractor and their related activities;
- The use, maintenance, and storage of all audit logs which are in place to monitor all types and kinds of physical activity;
- The controlling and management of any sort of physical access device.

The System and Communications Protection (SC) This practice area deals with the monitoring, controlling, and protection of all of the communications mechanisms that are deployed and in place in both the external and internal environments of either the contractor or the subcontractor.

The specific objectives here are to:

- If the external/internal communication boundaries have been clearly identified;
- The flow of communications are *monitored* at both the internal and external environments;
- The flow of communications are *controlled* at both the internal and external environments;
- The flow of communications are *protected* at both the internal and external environments.

It is important to note that communications also include the following:

- Gateways;
- Firewalls;
- Human Guards;
- Routers;
- Code analysis/Virtualization systems;
- Encrypted tunnels (such as Virtual Private Networks);
- Commercial telecommunications;

Other provisions that can be further examined in this area include the following:

- The physical or logical separation of IT and Network Infrastructures based upon by using Subnets.

The System and Information Integrity (SI)   The practice area deals with making sure that any errors in the IT and Network Infrastructure of a contractor or a subcontractor are properly documented, reported, and corrected in a very timely manner.

The primary objectives here are to:

- The time in which flaws or errors have been *identified* has been specified and corrected in the timeframe that has been established;
- The time in which flaws or errors have been *reported* has been specified and corrected in the timeframe that has been established;
- The time in which flaws or errors have been *corrected* has been specified and corrected in the timeframe that has been established.

Other statutes that can be further examined in this area include the following:

- What mechanisms are put into place to protect the organization of the contractor or subcontractor from malware or other types of malicious-based source code;
- The schedule and the procedures in which the relevant software patches and firmware upgrades are applied;
- The manner and ways in which the IT and Network Infrastructure are scanned when any type or kind of file is downloaded, opened, and if necessary executed.

Another Data Privacy Law that is also closely affiliated with the GDPR, CCPA, and the CMMS is that of the PCI-DSS. This is actually a consortium of the major credit companies to adopt a set of best standards and practices in order to protect the credit card information and data of the card holders.

The Background of the PCI-DSS

PCI-DSS is an acronym that stands for the Payment Card Industry Data Security Standard. It has been set forth by the major credit card companies such as Visa, Master Card, American Express, and

Discover in order to create and execute a common set of standards and best practices for businesses of all sizes to secure credit processing on behalf of their customers. The first version of this was passed on December 15th, 2004, with the latest one being released on May 2018.

Although the major credit card companies enforce the PCI-DSS, it is actually administered centrally through an organization known as the Payment Card Industry Security Standards Council.

The Compliance Levels of the PCI-DSS

At present, there are four levels of compliance, depending upon the volume of credit card transactions that a business processes on an annual basis. These can be described as follows:

1) Level 1

This level applies to those organizations that process 6 million or greater transactions per year. The business must be audited by an officer of the Council, and this has to be conducted at least once per year. On top of this, the business must also pass a test known as a "PCI Scan" that is administered by an Approved Scanning Vendor (also known as an "ASV") on a quarterly basis.

2) Level 2

This designed for those businesses that conduct in between 1 and 6 million credit card transactions per year. But rather than go through a comprehensive audit, organizations just have to submit a Self-Assessment Questionnaire (also known as the "SAQ"). Additionally, they may also be selected for a PCI Scan on a random basis.

3) Level 3

This particular level of compliance is targeting those entities that process in between 20,000 and 1 million credit card transactions yearly. Also, they do not have to undergo an audit, but they submit a lighter version of the SAQ, which is just an assessment of the Controls they have implemented to secure the credit card information and processing details. They may also be subject to a PCI Scan.

4) Level 4

This only applies to businesses that process under 20,000 credit card transactions per year. The compliance requirements are the same as for Level 3.

The Requirements of the PCI-DSS

For those businesses that are subject to the PCI-DSS, there are 12 security requirements that they must implement and enforce. This is an addition to being compliant for the respective level that they are presently at. These requirements are as follows:

1) The Use of Network Security Devices

This includes the deployment of firewalls, routers, and network intrusion devices close by to wherever the credit card of the customer is being processed.

2) Making Use of Robust Passwords

The passwords that are created must be long and complex enough so that they are difficult to crack at the first attempt. The use of a password manager is strongly encouraged to create and enforce these kinds of passwords.

3) Protecting Credit Card Numbers

The use of encryption to scramble the credit card numbers is required so that they remain in a useless state even if they were to be intercepted by a Cyberattacker.

4) The Lines of Communication Must Be Made Secure

Whenever credit card numbers and relevant data are transmitted, the network lines of communications through which this occurs must also be encrypted as well.

5) The Usage of Anti-Virus Software

The Point of Sale (PoS) terminals as well as other devices that come into interaction with the actual credit card must have anti-virus software installed onto them, and they must be kept updated with the latest software on a timely basis.

6) All Devices Must Be Protected

In addition to that stated in #5, all other devices that are used to safeguard the credit card information and transaction either directly or indirectly must also have anti-virus software installed onto them and must be also be kept updated.

7) <u>Access to Data Must Be Severely Restricted</u>

Anybody who has to have access to credit card information/data must be ascertained on a need to know basis. Anybody who does not need to have access to it (especially external, third parties) should be given any rights or permissions to do so under any circumstance.

8) <u>Unique IDs Must Be Established</u>

For those parties that need to have access to the credit card data must have their own ID that is specifically created for this very reason. The use of the same ID for multiple entities is strictly prohibited.

9) <u>All Storage Mediums Should Be Securely Stored</u>

Any kind or type of device that is used to store credit card numbers and other relevant data (whether it is in a physical or digital form) must remain locked in a secure area at the place of the business. In this regard, access should also be heavily restricted as well.

10) <u>Accurate Records Must Be Kept</u>

Any credit card transactions that take place must be thoroughly documented and archived for a certain number of reviews, for both compliance and audit-related purposes.

11) <u>Testing for Vulnerabilities</u>

Any environment that processes or stores credit information/data must be tested on a regular basis for any unknown vulnerabilities that could exist. This can be primarily done through penetration testing and/or threat hunting.

12) <u>Creating a Security Policy</u>

A specific and dedicated security policy must be crafted and strictly enforced for any of those businesses that fall into the four types of level categories, as reviewed in the last section.

Notes

1 https://www.itgovernance.co.uk/cyber-resilience
2 https://www.cisecurity.org/blog/cyber-extortion-an-industry-hot-topic/
3 https://www.propertyinsurancecoveragelaw.com/2012/12/articles/insurance/are-you-covered-sublimits-can-sneak-up-on-unaware-policyholders/
4 https://www.baesystems.com/en/cybersecurity/feature/the-nation-state-actor
5 CMMC Assessment Guide: Version 1.10, November 2020

Index

Page numbers in **bold** indicate tables.

Printed in the United States
by Baker & Taylor Publisher Services